First published 2013 by Elliott and Thompson Limited
27 John Street, London WC1N 2BX
www.eandtbooks.com

ISBN: 978-1-90965-313-9

Project editor: Jeannette Ballantyne
Cover design by Jem Butcher
Interior design by James Collins

We'd like to credit the following photographers:

Harold Baruch, Alex Harvey Brown, Tim Evan-Cook, Sarah Dunn/www.sarahdunn.com, Chris Evans, Anthony Flach, Edmund Flach, Sebastian Gonzalez, Lex Hallaby, Maria Hobbs, Adam Holt, Laura Jamson, Antonia Jater, Jeff Jessop, Liz Kitchen, Vera Klokova, Laraine Krantz, Michael Le Poer Trench, Joe Lewis, Keith Lillis, James Mason, Doug McKenzie, Zöe Norfolk, Rowan O'Duffy, Femi Omole, John Pridmore, Ralph Rapley, RHWL Arts Team/John Walson, Anne-Marie Sanderson, Sebastian Sardou, Gabor Scott, Brian Shuel, Ian Smith, David Steen, Rob Ware, Christopher Wells, Lorna Yabsley/Bang Wallop, Rachel Yates. Image on p. 6 courtesy of Wrotham Park.

Every effort has been made to trace copyright holders for photographs used within this book. Where this has not been possible, the publisher will be happy to credit them in future editions.

Garden Sculpture designed by Bryan Parkes
Chickenshed logo designed by Sal Shuel

Printed in Italy by Printer Trento

MAX AND JANE RAYNE *were inspired by the work of Jo Collins and Mary Ward in Chickenshed's early days. From 1988, when they first met Chickenshed, Max and Jane became trustees. Max was chairman and Jane became president and formed a fundraising committee to raise money to build the theatre in Southgate.*

Today, Natasha Rayne continues the Rayne family's strong commitment to the charity. The Trustees of the Rayne Foundation wish all involved every success for the future and thank them for the work they are doing.

The Rayne Foundation

CONTENTS

Dame Judi Dench.

FOREWORD

I FIRST SAW CHICKENSHED in 1985. I was astounded by the ability displayed. Then came the understanding that not all the performers were conventionally able. It was an astonishing moment. The effort and the commitment by the performers was entrancing. I felt immediately that we should encourage and support the people who were making this happen. After all, if this can be achieved in performance then probably it can be achieved in any activity. Chickenshed could change everyone's perception of each other, which would surely lead to a better, more comfortable world.

I felt that if I could just persuade Jane and Max Rayne to see them perform then things would happen. I think they probably came reluctantly to a leaky church hall on a Sunday evening, but they were won over and pitched in with such energy and commitment that success was inevitable. In retrospect, I suppose it all happened very quickly after that, greatly helped by the Princess of Wales. She gave everyone splendid support and encouragement – and of course she put Chickenshed on the front pages.

Nevertheless, it seems incredible to be celebrating forty years of Chickenshed. I've seen so many productions, seen the lives of so many young people changed and enhanced by the work Jo and Mary and their team have accomplished. It has indeed been 'an awfully big adventure' – and long may it continue.

Judi Dench

Jo Collins and Mary Ward.

INTRODUCTION

FOR MANY YEARS people have said to us, 'You must tell your story' – to which we have always replied, 'Yes, we must!' But it was only when one of our long-standing parents and volunteers, Wendy Sharer, came to us and virtually knocked down our office door in her enthusiasm that we finally did something about it.

We felt that our story would best be told not just in words but also in pictures. We have had some of the most wonderful photographers over the years (see page ii for credits). These photographs – a small selection of which are displayed here – have captured the very spirit and essence of our work.

For us to actually write this book would, we also felt, be an almost impossible task. So we approached a long-time friend whose work we admired, Liz Thomson, to write it from her perspective using interviews and fre-quent visits to the theatre to observe our work. She has been connected to Chickenshed from its very early days and so aware of our journey, but not personally involved. To our delight she accepted the challenge – the fruits of which are within. We are so pleased that she did.

There are many, many people whose faith, love and commitment to Chickenshed over the years we would like to acknowledge. Many are mentioned in this book, but not all. We know we cannot possibly thank all of these exceptional individuals by name, but we have at-tempted to encapsulate the different groups and pay tribute to them at the end of the book (see page 246). You know who you are!

Jo Collins and Mary Ward,
co-founders of Chickenshed

THE FIRST TIME I saw a Chickenshed performance was over a decade ago. The stage was packed with kids from every conceivable walk of life – singing, dancing, and acting their hearts out – and the experience left me profoundly touched and inspired. I left Southgate that night wanting to do what I could for this unique charity.

Over the years my involvement has gone from being a donor to fundraiser to proud parent of two young cast members – and most recently chairman of the Board of Trustees.

From its early, humble beginnings to a charity of significant standing today, Chickenshed has provided a sense of purpose and a creative outlet for tens of thousands of young people – to express themselves, interact with and learn from their peers in ways they probably never thought possible.

'That's the way the world should be,' a friend said recently after seeing his first Chickenshed performance.

So true. Chickenshed changes and enhances not only the lives of the young people benefiting from its programmes, but also those of parents and audience members.

Thanks to the dedication and pioneering spirit of Jo, Mary and their talented teams over these forty years, Chickenshed today encompasses – in addition to the groundbreaking inclusive Theatre the charity is renowned for – nationally accredited education courses, impressive community outreach activities, a dynamic new branch in Kensington and Chelsea (whose performances Jake and Noah Berger ensure I never miss), and twenty-one further satellite 'Sheds' including two in Russia.

I feel immensely privileged to be contributing to this magnificent organisation and, as Chickenshed moves into its fifth decade, we are working hard to ensure it is around for another forty years and beyond – touching the lives of as many people as possible.

Josh Berger, chairman of Chickenshed

Josh Berger.

ACT 1
A BRIGHTER DREAM

IT WAS CARL JUNG who suggested that multiple meaningful occurrences – synchronicities – are responsible for bringing people and events into our lives at just the right moment. Deeper than mere coincidences, synchronicities are spiritual and psychological experiences which, if we are open to them – if we are willing to trust our intuition – push us in new and unexpected directions, enabling us to make a connection with something greater than our individual selves. Those who believe in synchronicity believe there is more to everyone than meets the eye.

If synchronicity has been a shaping force in the history of Chickenshed Theatre, so too have been dreams. Not so much the signs and symbols of Jungian analysis, but of people with a shared vision and in whom the dreams of so many hundreds of others gradually became invested. For Jo Collins, Anthony Filby, Peter and Sally Heath, and Mary Ward – whose vision inspired a company that now has some 800 members and a waiting list twice that long, whose players have performed on stages in the West End, in Edinburgh and beyond, and in front of innumerable royals and Oscar-winning actors – had a dream of something that was beyond most people's imagination. Four decades on, despite the exposure and the awards, what Chickenshed does – putting people of all ages and all abilities on stage together – remains incomprehensible to many, even those who watched the triumph of so many Paralympians in London 2012.

'It sounds arrogant, but there's no doubt the Paralympics' ceremony was influenced by Chickenshed,' Jo ventures, as she and Mary sit chatting in the Theatre's recording studio, having watched the preview of *Sleeping Beauty*, the company's 2012 Christmas show. Adds Mary: 'We have set precedents. We've learned from the children we've taught.'

PREVIOUS PAGE
The original
chicken shed.

LEFT
Mary and Jo
at a workshop
in the original
chicken shed.

But while Chickenshed's influence may be visible on stage and off, while what they do may have shaped decisions taken and legislation written far from its north London base, Chickenshed Theatre remains unique. To some people that would be a welcome accolade. To the founders, it is a disappointment. For much as they feel a great sense of pride in what they have achieved, a part of their dream remains unrealised: the opportunities offered by Chickenshed shouldn't be unique – they should be universal.

The story of what would prove a genuinely life-changing encounter – life-changing for the principals, and for the thousands of people who have passed through Chickenshed – began on 4 February 1974. Jo was in the church hall at Vita et Pax in Oakwood, teaching guitar to some of the kids who attended Junior Youth Club, which Anthony helped run. Mary, who had recently moved into the area, was introduced. 'We just clicked,' Jo remembers. It was the first of those many coincidences: the previous owner of the home into which the Ward family had recently moved was also Catholic and had told Mary to be sure to go to Vita et Pax, recommending the folk mass from which *Rock* – a musical based, like *Godspell* and *Jesus Christ Superstar*, on the Gospels – had sprung as a particularly good way to meet people. In fact, Mary had already been and was 'very struck' by both the folk mass and the lead singer-guitarist. As she and Jo met for the first time, she quickly realised that 'we were on the same wavelength. We started talking about performing. Jo had had this great experience and I'd developed a love of performance. We talked about how wonderful it would be to develop that and, right from the beginning, we talked about starting our own company.'

Jo and Mary quickly recognised that if they were to fulfil the ambitious plans they were incubating, a proper rehearsal space was needed. 'We'd been rehearsing in the church hall and it was getting increasingly frustrating – we had to be out before the Guides and not make a noise during Mass, not move the piano. It was very limiting,' Jo remembers, 'and Mary said "If *only* we could find premises. A barn would be great." I reminded her about Lady Elizabeth Byng, who'd come to see every single performance of *Rock*. She was a landowner, and I said I'd go and see her – I was sure she'd love the work to continue.'

Lady Elizabeth presided over the 2,500-acre estate of Wrotham Park, just a few miles up the road in Barnet. A neo-Palladian pile built in 1754 for Admiral John Byng, it's now popular with film directors – scenes from

Top left: The Vita et Pax church in Oakwood, north London.

Bottom left: Early workshop with Teresa Heaney.

Right: Lady Elizabeth Byng, owner of the original chicken shed.

Vanity Fair, *Jane Eyre* and *Bridget Jones's Diary* were shot there – and when Jo first visited she was invited to take tea in the dining room, now familiar from *Gosford Park*. 'She could only afford to heat one room and she opened the door wearing several jumpers, an overcoat and Wellington boots. But she had a maid, and the sideboard was laid out with beautiful napery, and China tea, India tea, coffee, scones, all different types of jam – just for the two of us!

'She asked if we were going to do *Rock* again, and I explained that we wanted to do more things like it, but the problem was that the church hall was off-limits and what could we do? She asked how she could help and I said we'd like a barn and did she have anything on any of her farms. "I've got *just* the very thing – a *chicken shed*." I didn't even know what a chicken shed was and I thought she'd lost it a bit, but I humoured her and she suggested we go and see it there and then.'

Lady Elizabeth drove her bright yellow BMW 'like an absolute maniac' down a winding road to her farm, where stood three wartime sheds. 'What about this?' she asked, showing Jo inside one of them, its dirt floor strewn with straw and feathers. 'I said it would be brilliant – but how much? And she said we could have it, though of course there was no paperwork. We were there for several years until she died.'

"What we need is a big barn in the country where we can just do our own thing..."

MARY WARD

With help from friends, parents and young thespians, all trace of chickens was soon banished: a floor was laid, the inside painted. The burgeoning drama group now had a home. 'The kids would say, "We're going to the chicken shed" – and the name just stuck.' Now they could rock the joint.

JUMP CUT, FLASHBACK, REWIND … Who *were* these people? What had led them to embark on this awfully big adventure?

What they shared was a love of music and theatre, and, as it happened, a religion, Roman Catholicism, but their lives had taken somewhat different courses. Mary had embraced school and had followed what was clearly her vocation: to teach. Jo, who can't remember a time when she wasn't singing, wanted to make music and own a restaurant. She was a less easy fit in the classroom. Then there was Anthony, who studied first human biology and then music which, when it came time to support a family, led him to leave Chickenshed and go into school teaching. Peter and Sally Heath, he a City University engineering lecturer, she a maths teacher, were a bohemian couple, always eager to engage in something new and exciting, despite the demands of their large family. Sally could always be relied upon to paint the big picture, while Peter revealed an ability to turn a clever lyric.

An only child born lateish into the lives of a civil servant and a headmistress, Mary quickly developed a love of performance, though she did not herself crave the spotlight. Her mother took her to the ballet – Sadler's Wells and Covent Garden – which had a profound effect: 'The *overwhelmingness* of it. I loved the way it took you in and the whole audience became part of the spectacle.' Her mother's teaching was also a major influence. The first head of a new primary school in Ilford, Doris O'Dwyer taught in ways which were atypical of the 1950s. Mary, who went to school elsewhere but was sometimes allowed to accompany her mother, remembers: 'Every morning children were allowed to do what they liked in the classroom, while in the afternoon it was made more formal. She also taught me how important every individual is and that is one of the things I carried into *my* teaching and then into Chickenshed: the fact that there isn't an individual who can't teach us something, so every individual needs to be listened to

and developed and watched and learned from. The older kids and the younger kids worked together on various things and that developed a relationship between them which meant there was a softness in the school.' That, too, is part of the Chickenshed approach. 'Really, it was from my mum that I got the feel of the way you do it.'

Before Chickenshed, however, Mary also taught conventionally, having first studied drama and history at Digby Stuart College, now part of the University of Roehampton: 'I taught in Ilford for about seven years and we made drama happen at school.' It was a mixed area with problem children, kids with no solid home background who, for whatever reason, often had difficulty reading. So it was very empowering for them to discover that they could be taught their lines and stand on stage next to classmates able to read their own and feel part of a tight-knit group: 'I saw early on that drama could make a real difference to children who were disadvantaged.'

In those days, of course, dyslexia and autism – though named and identified – were rarely diagnosed, so it's almost inevitable that some of those 'problem' children were battling against the odds without any of

LEFT
Mary Ward, artistic director
of Chickenshed.

BELOW
Peter and Sally Heath, co-writers
of the musical *Rock*.

"There isn't an individual who can't teach us something, so every individual needs to be listened to and learned from."

MARY WARD

the help available to sufferers and their parents today. 'I can't remember identifying who was dyslexic and who was autistic in my teaching. I just remember knowing, like my mother, that every individual had something to teach us, so I made sure that I gave time to each and every one of them.' Mary also remembers making a mistake while explaining something in a lesson and then apologising for her error: 'A couple of boys, who were really difficult and full of trouble, came up to me afterwards and said, "That was brilliant, because you said you were wrong, and teachers *never* say they're wrong." Somehow it seemed to establish a relationship between us, that I would always tell them the truth. And I thought, *I must remember that. I must always stick to what's right and what's true* – because it really affected them. I *loved* teaching, *absolutely loved it*. It was a real joy to me. Even now, if I go into primary schools, I remember the feeling.'

Outside the classroom, Mary worked at the Redbridge Theatre Workshop with the local drama advisor. As they would be at Chickenshed, everyone was welcome and she remembers putting on *Oh! What a Lovely War*, which Joan Littlewood had made such a success down the road at Stratford East a few years earlier.

In the 1960s, marriage and motherhood inevitably meant a career break, and, when Mary returned to work, it was to Barnet College, where she used drama as therapy for a group of older men from a home and with some 'challenging' youngsters: 'I was trying to get them to talk, to be creative with a bit of language. They were *so* under-stimulated.'

For Jo, the path was somewhat different, though as the crow flies, she's travelled a short distance indeed. Born a few hundred yards down the road from where the Theatre now stands, she is the younger of two children and the family's only cradle Catholic. There was a piano at home, and both parents were musical, though Jo learned only recently that her mother, Nora, who performed during the war years, had been invited to audition by one of the big-band leaders of the day but was thwarted by her elder sister, 'who *totally* disapproved. She could have been a performer. She had a great voice, really good – Marlene Dietrich without the accent.' At seventy-eight, Nora would pick up the threads of her performing career, doing a turn in the Chickenshed bar on 'Jo Collins and Friends' nights.

Naturally, then, Jo was not discouraged from singing (indeed, she sang all the time, standing up for a solo on

LEFT
Jo Collins, director of music
at Chickenshed.

BELOW
Jo performing at Chickenshed.

her first day at school) and, though she didn't like practising scales, persisted with piano lessons. From an early age, she was making up songs: 'I was an entrepreneur as well as a performer. I did a musical in my own house when I was about five. Two friends played all the bit parts and I played all the main parts. It was called *Caveman's Troubles* [inspired, of course, by *The Flintstones*]. I wrote the script, directed it, made the tickets with my John Bull printing set, sold them to all the neighbours.' At the age of ten, she made her own guitar, 'though it ended up more like a balalaika because I couldn't work out how to bend the wood. I put a neck on, glued the bits together, made pegs, bought strings … I had no idea about chord shapes so I made my own fingerings.' She won the first talent contest she entered, aged eleven: 'The prize was a *massive* embroidery kit, which I absolutely *hated*.'

At secondary school it was a different story. Beyond formal music lessons, Jo was actively *dis*couraged. 'I used to bring guitars into school, and drums, and they always got confiscated because it was the Devil's music in those days. The teachers were all nuns. I left at sixteen, the minute I could, but before leaving I got a band together and we did a gig. That was all right because we were raising money. On the last day of school I went home on the bus carrying all the instruments I'd reclaimed.'

Jo wanted to sing, but recognised that it was a precarious lifestyle. Besides, she had a secondary ambition, no more secure – to own a restaurant. 'I was always on stage. I played around the folk clubs, started one in the Finchley Road with my best friend from school. But I thought, *I'll never make a living from it. I've got to have something to fall back on.*' So she took a National Diploma in hotel management and catering at Hendon Polytechnic: 'I hated it and as soon as I'd qualified I just went out and sang. I joined a band, I went on tour, I went on cruises, I sang with big bands, and I got a job in Germany, singing country 'n' western on the American bases. My parents were worried, but they let me do it.'

Though she would later open a wine bar, Jo never did have to fall back on her catering skills – for twenty years she made a living singing, playing four or five gigs a week, sometimes just with a guitar (five or six bookings a night on New Year's Eve), sometimes with a dance band ('a bit soulless; you had to do it exactly as written'). In a world where supply inevitably outstrips demand, her ability quickly to learn a song and sing a harmony line meant she soon acquired a reputation not only for live gigs but as a session singer able to lay down a backing vocal, or record a commercial, with the minimum of studio time: 'I can hear a song and immediately

know what the chords are, more than I can know all the words. Bob Dylan, Joan Baez, Stevie Wonder, the Beatles … to be brought up on that kind of music is just such a silver spoon in the mouth. I feel so privileged to have been at the record-buying age when the Beatles released their first single. I couldn't *wait* to get down the record shop. I saw them at the Finsbury Park Astoria, but I couldn't hear them for all the screaming and that annoyed me – I wanted to *listen*.'

Caught up in the Devil's music though she might have been, Jo still went to Mass. Now, though, she went through a period of doubt, but when she heard that Vita et Pax had started 'a pop mass', she thought she'd check it out: 'I went for the music, not because I believed in God. I stood at the back of the church and I heard this flute player. I thought, *He's good.*'

The flute player was Anthony, still at school: quiet, serious, somewhat intense; an unlikely looking Pete Townsend fan who played guitar left-handed. A local boy with one sister born on his tenth birthday, he had been an altar server and sang in local choirs, but he didn't start learning the flute until secondary school, where he was fortunate to have an inspirational music teacher who taught him about harmony and counter-

point way ahead of his classmates. Despite his obvious talents, he was 'expected' to be either a doctor or a scientist, and duly studied human biology at Chelsea College, his parents having agreed that, if music still called, they would support him through a second degree. Thus, having gained his BSc and after a year out to take music A-Level, he went to City University, following that with a year's teaching certificate at Middlesex and a probationary year at a local school. Each course was carefully selected so he could live at home (rare in those halcyon days of student grants) in order to continue writing with Jo.

As a teenager, Anthony remembers learning 'all these religious pop songs' from a young man back from America, where he was training for the priesthood: 'Somebody, probably I, wrote them down. One of them was "Lord of the Dance" and we performed it on my sixteenth birthday, 25 October 1968, at the High Mass, which was in the evening.' Jo, whom he'd met a few months earlier, was among the congregation. From somewhere, Anthony can't remember where, came the idea of 'a folk mass', quite radical in those days, with the Latin liturgy only recent history and 'happy-clappy' music the preserve of American Baptists: 'Jo

FAR LEFT
Anthony Filby, co-writer of *Rock*.

LEFT
Top: Anthony conducting *Rock*. Musicians include Ian Revens and Stuart Curtis on saxophone, and Steve Sidwell on trumpet.

Bottom: Anthony composing and playing guitar.

wasn't involved in the first group mass, but, a couple of weeks later, I heard these drums behind me and I turned round and saw her.' It didn't take long before she would step forward as the lead singer-guitarist.

Soon, the two young musicians were writing new music to the traditional words of the Catholic liturgy, to Psalms and to prayers, encouraged by Dom Edmund Jones, a thoughtful and forward-looking monk much in demand by the BBC. Indeed, he quickly began commissioning Jo and Anthony to write music for his spots on Radio 4. 'I remember he phoned me up about nine o'clock one night and asked if I knew St Francis' Canticle to the Sun, and would I be able to set it to music,' Jo says. Only after accepting the commission was she told she'd be performing it live at seven the next morning! Anthony came over, and together they worked out the flute part. 'It was a real roaster, and I didn't get any sleep. But it was *Pick of the Week* and then part of *Pick of the Year*, so that was a bit of an accolade.' It led to a series of Sunday-morning broadcasts for the duo, many of them featuring traditional hymns alongside hits of the day, such as Paul Simon's 'I Am a Rock'. There was also a TV show, broadcast from Pebble Mill, for which they wrote four songs based around the Parables.

It was through such writing that Jo regained her faith: 'I learned that I wrote my best music when I was writing with a spiritual meaning. Previously, I'd been writing pop songs – I'd actually got a publishing deal with Chappell, but nothing got taken up and I was getting very disillusioned. Then I started setting the Psalms, which everyone said were beautiful, and I realised that when words are meaningful and have soul to them it connects with my musicality and brings out the best in me. I didn't know I sang them with such conviction, but I did, apparently, and it happened in that subliminally spiritual way that I began to get my faith back.'

THUS WAS THE WAY PAVED for *Rock*, a cleverly succinct title which spoke at once to Catholics ('upon this rock I will build my church') and to those who worshipped at the altar of rock 'n' roll – indeed, 'God rock', as it was referred to at the time, was proving that the Devil did not, after all, have all the best tunes. It was 1972: after the hedonism of *Hair* and *Oh! Calcutta!*, Jesus had made his West End (and Broadway) debut, first in *Godspell*, then in *Jesus Christ Superstar*, the latter marking the beginning of the Tim Rice and Andrew Lloyd-Webber hegemony. Dom Edmund, an English Benedictine, liked the raw honesty of the former

ROCK

but disliked the razzmatazz of the latter. 'It was the difference between going to Westminster Cathedral and going to your local church. He was *absolutely obsessed* with *Godspell* and was always looking for people to take to see it,' Jo recalls. 'He was going on about it *so* much that Anthony and I said we could write something like it. Sally and Peter wrote the script and we wrote the music, and we did it in church. He gave it *such* a big press and everybody came.

'I'll *never* forget the first performance. I'd never played in a theatrical setting before and I didn't understand the multi-layers that you could have, as opposed to just playing music. I'd only ever done concerts or gigs. Having other people sing your music was just wonderful. I directed it, more or less, and a few other people helped out. I remember going home that night, *so* high. I kept phoning people. I couldn't stop talking about the effect it had on me. The buzz, the applause, the audience reaction – it was just *unbelievable*. I said, "We've *got* to do this again." Jo's and Anthony's fathers each paid £100 towards the cost of a demo recording, made by Alan O'Duffy, who'd played Jesus but who in his day job was a sound engineer who'd won a gold disc for his work on the studio recording of *Jesus Christ Superstar.* Another coincidence. Alan introduced the pair to Dave Dee of Atlantic Records, who liked the

LEFT
Rock at Vita et Pax.

Bottom left:
Alan O'Duffy as Jesus (left) and Mark Haines as Peter (right).

ABOVE
Jo Collins, Anthony Filby, and Peter and Sally Heath in publicity photographs from the early days of *Rock.*

Left: Dom Placid with Jo and Mary on the way to a special ceremony conducted to 'bless the land' on which the Theatre was to be built.

Top middle: Dom Placid Meylink.

Top right: Harry and Nora Collins.

Bottom right: Stan and Peggy Filby. Stan was company secretary of River Island clothing company, which he brought in as an early sponsor.

melodies though was less keen on the words – God rock was giving way to glam rock – but said he'd give it another listen if Jo and Anthony rewrote them.

The moment passed, the year turned. Anthony, now studying for his first degree, was chairman of the members' committee of the youth club which required that he attend not only the Sunday-night meeting but also Monday's junior version. It was there that he met Angela Morton, whom he would later marry, and he was there with Jo the night Mary came by, encouraged along by another priest, Dom Placid Meylink, who hoped to draw on her expertise as a primary-school teacher. Jo recalls: 'The first thing she said to me was, "Cardinal Heenan is my godfather." And I said, "Well, I wrote *Rock*."' Mary, with just a hint of embarrassment, refutes the anecdote, though Cardinal Heenan, Archbishop of Westminster from 1963 until his death in 1975, was indeed her godfather, a long-time family friend who, as a parish priest in London's Forest Gate, had married her parents. Anthony, the co-writer of *Rock* to whom Jo immediately introduced Mary, remembers discussing politics and the burning question of the day, on which Prime Minister Edward Heath would shortly call an election: *who runs Britain?*

According to Anthony, 'Dom Placid was a great influence on Jo *and* Mary because he harped on about how everyone's got special needs. Whether you're shy or confident, that's a special need that requires handling. We're all individuals. And that was a great influence when I went into teaching.' Angela – who learned to make costumes with couture-trained Joy Hollick, whose son Graham would later pick up the mantle – recalls Mary as 'the charismatic leader', Jo as 'very upfront' and Anthony as 'this very quiet person who seemed to write lots of music'. The three immediately hit it off and recognised how well their skills and talents fitted together. With Sally and Peter Heath, older in years but young in spirit, the team was complete.

That Monday-night encounter soon bore fruit: *Isaac*, a half-hour drama with music co-written by Jo and Anthony but this time directed by Mary, about the sacrifice of Abraham's only son. Among the musicians drafted in for the occasion were guitarists Kevin Savigar, who went on to work with Rod Stewart, and Laurence Juber, who worked briefly with Wings before forging a unique path as a soloist. The embryonic theatre company had not yet been named, not quite, but in retrospect it's possible to see that *Isaac* marked the birth of Chickenshed. Appropriately, given the occasion on which it made its debut – the Easter Vigil, a celebration of new life.

Buoyed up by the success of that first shared endeavour, the pied pipers would lead the youth drama group

RIGHT
An early rehearsal in
the chicken shed, with
Brian Hanrahan and
Mary taking the lead.

to their new home in Wrotham Park, where everyone mucked in to get the place ready. The DIY skills of Peter Heath were put to particularly good use. A pipe-smoking hippy paterfamilias with a large family, he always found time for other kids, who'd pile into the back of his open-top Triumph Vitesse. 'This group of four people – Jo, Mary, Anthony and Peter – used to hold it all together and run rehearsals in the freezing-cold winter,' Angela continues. They would become Chickenshed's first directors. Anthony's father Stan, an accountant, later became treasurer and would bring in River Island, of which he was company secretary, as an early sponsor. At the early shows, he and his wife Peggy were always to be found on the door, taking ticket money.

The chicken shed became a place to hang out, a place where nobody was judged and everyone felt safe, older members looking after younger ones. There were parties of course ('The couple who lived near the entrance were very patient, despite seventy people turning up on a Saturday night'), Peter's home brew paid for via an honesty box, but also a great deal of hard work. *Chrysalis* was the first production to come out of the new space.

'Our principal motivation wasn't religion,' Anthony reflects. 'There was inevitably a spiritual aspect to it, but it wasn't specifically Catholic – it was a church with a big social side to it. Chickenshed became a lifestyle. The music was binding. Honesty and trust was built up and that, and working together, created a phenomenal bond. Anyone there for their own ego was very difficult to deal with. There was no status – everyone was as important as everyone else.'

Chrysalis, 1975.

MAEVE GILL

MAEVE GILL was twelve when she joined Chickenshed: 'I've always loved dancing though I'm not particularly good at it.' What she hadn't expected was 'the social, emotional value-based dimension – I thought it would be an after-school club and theatre. It was hard at first because I didn't know anyone, but there was something drawing me to this experience. I remember loving the philosophy as soon as I arrived. And I always wanted to go, though sometimes it was pressurised when there was such a short time to rehearse.'

She had little prior experience of disability but learnt quickly that each person had their own unique set of abilities to contribute to every performance. At the beginning, Maeve agrees she must have worried about how to act, but 'now I recognise that everyone has differing strengths and weaknesses – some are just more immediately visible than others'. Of course, she was in a variety of shows and loved 'the physicality, the unspoken trust and teamwork, the amazing connection when you're synchronised in movement. It's an experience I've only had with Chickenshed.'

What made a profound impression was Maeve's role as a support worker for Children's Theatre. She remembers Adrian, an Eastern European orphan aged

> ## "Chickenshed played a huge part in the person I've become."

around five who had just been adopted: 'He was extremely traumatised and his mum explained that he didn't have any neurological dysfunction, but the trauma meant he didn't speak or engage. I spent six months working with him every week and we grew to have a kind of unspoken bond. I remember at Christmas his mum gave me a card and a candle, which I still have, and explained what an impact our relationship had had. He would look excited coming in the door, smiling rather than clinging to his mum. There was a change in his level of engagement.' Maeve admits to having been 'very scared' at the outset: 'There's no way to teach you, you have to learn by doing, but there's great support and by then I had a strong sense of Chickenshed values. You had to experiment, take risks, see what worked.'

Maeve left the Theatre to study psychology at Oxford, though she's never broken the connection. Much of her career has been spent in the Home Office and she brought her team to 'as the mother of a brown boy ...': 'It was such an important show, I wanted to share it with them.'

Right now, she's embarked on a Masters in positive psychology, which looks at people's strengths and helps them flourish. 'Chickenshed', Maeve sums up, 'played a huge part in the person I've become.'

RIGHT Maeve Gill.

FAR RIGHT Maeve performing in *Pinocchio*, 2001.

HANNAH DE SPON

ASKED WHAT LED her into animation, Hannah de Spon explains that she 'watched a lot of cartoons with my sister Louise and never grew out of it'. Her tastes run the gamut from Disney to Pixar, but her preference is for 'hand-drawn and British'.

Hannah works for Karrot Animation, currently on *Sarah and Duck*, CBeebies' series for preschoolers. She's been there three years and previously taught animation, everything from flickbooks to Macs. Would she be doing all this if not for Chickenshed? 'I don't know if I'd be doing it as *effectively*. Chickenshed opened my eyes to different ways of looking at things. It made me more objective – I can see both sides. It taught me to be critical of my own views.'

Hannah's first encounter with the company was at the Enfield Town Show. Her mother asked if she'd like to explore further and they went to see *The Night Before Christmas* at The Place. 'It was a really stunning performance and I wanted to be part of it. I joined when I was

seven.' Louise, now part of Total Ensemble, an inclusive company in Norfolk, joined at five.

In addition to acting, Hannah recalls composing songs and creating artwork: 'We'd be waiting in the dressing rooms to go on and I'd draw sketches and comics, which other people seemed to like. It helped to have willing performers happy to pose for sketches! I think that's how Paul Morrall picked up the idea of doing artwork for Tales from the Shed. Confidence and encouragement with regards to artistic skills were two of

the most important things Chickenshed gave me. It was a nice environment, fun and not formal. You weren't judged for doing stuff wrong.' Occasionally she worked as group leader: 'It was fascinating to see how quickly kids became inclusive. It was so natural. Chickenshed doesn't mollycoddle people; it just says *we're all in this together.*'

Memories stand out: 'The Golden Jubilee – I was photographed next to the Queen – a peace festival in Hyde Park on the hottest day of the year, the Albert Hall, and *The Night Before Christmas*. Even today the songs get stuck in my head.'

Hannah reflects: 'What I gained from Chickenshed was confidence, not being afraid to speak out, which is quite a big deal. You can't be shy – you get over it and you enjoy the excitement of performing and the nerves it gives you, the energy. I've applied that to my work. I put that energy into the characters I'm animating.'

ABOVE AND RIGHT Hannah de Spon (right) and at work (above).

Act 2
A PLACE OF OUR OWN

BY SUMMER 1974, the thirty or so teenagers who comprised what would shortly be known as Chickenshed were finally able to rehearse as and when they pleased. *Chrysalis*, created by Jo and Anthony, and Sally and Peter, and directed by Mary, was followed by *Alice*, which marked the group's first production in a theatre, the Intimate in nearby Palmers Green, once part of Britain's repertory circuit. Mary worked on the script, helped by a young Brian Hanrahan, while Jo and Anthony set Charles Lutwidge Dodgson's original poems. As its reputation grew, so did the company, and in 1976 a junior drama group was launched, mostly siblings of existing members.

Meanwhile, as their composing partnership continued to flourish, at Mary's suggestion Jo and Anthony set up Colby Music. Its purpose was to publish all the music written for the Mass – prayers, Psalms, songs for feast days – which found a ready market in churches across the land, as well as the scores of Chickenshed shows and smaller-scale musicals written specifically for schools. There were around twenty-four publications in all, and the operation ran initially from Mary's front room, later from Anthony's family home and, finally, from his own flat where, on Saturdays, Chickenshed teenagers earned double the M&S rate, plus a Big Mac, despatching thousands of orders. It was a well-oiled production line: Anthony and Jo wrote the music, separately and together, with the former copying the notes and the latter typing the words. With the help of a friendly local printer, Angela used her art and design skills to put it all together, a process which, in that far-off pre-digital age, involved scissors and cow gum. 'It was a huge success,' Anthony remembers. 'I had the loft converted specially and my dad put up shelves. Orders came in by the sackful. We had great fun, though now I can see it was a terrible fire risk – we all smoked in those days.'

by the likes of Gary Numan and the Hollies) were co-opted by Jo, believes that 'everyone had their own personal issues, if they're being honest. I didn't dislike it, but I did find it awkward and intimidating to start with. But at the end of a session you could see what a difference it had made.' He recalls one particular workshop: 'We were doing an improvisation and there was this girl with Down's and she was very, very awkward and she looked very, very grumpy. The idea was that you're at home and someone knocks on the door and they're going to ask you something and you have to respond to them in the way you feel. A Chickenshed member knocked on the imaginary door and asked "Do you want to buy a whippet?" Well, how *do* you respond to that? And she said, "*F*** off, I don't want your bloody whippets," and slammed the door in his face. We all just screeched with laughter and clapped. It was brilliant, *exactly* right.' Continues Francis, who is now a successful film composer, 'What we discovered was that it wasn't wrong to laugh. She was grinning from ear to ear – *she'd made people laugh, we were clapping her.* She'd never said a word – been coming for about six weeks. Then to say that – we were just on the floor.'

That was one breakthrough, but it wasn't easy and a decision was taken to split Wednesday Group activity into under-sixteens and over-sixteens. 'That made an immediate difference,' says Mary, as did the seconding of Janet Leach, a member of the Cheviots team who had studied drama at university.

The new members had a range of problems, some of which (like Down's, cerebral palsy, autism) had names. Others had suffered abuse or were slow learners or had behavioural problems. As the months passed and everyone involved gained confidence, so the group cohered, run now much like any drama group. 'So why was it separate? What were the reasons we wouldn't put these kids with their peer group and do away with special groups?' Mary remembers asking. The original Chickenshedders thought it was cool ('At all times, Chickenshed has to be *cool*; it's not a do-gooding place,' Jo emphasises) and were so keen to belong that they were happy to go in whatever direction they were taken. As the Wednesday Group dissolved and became simply another Chickenshed gathering, 'inclusive theatre' was born, its members organised according to age rather than ability.

SO WHAT EXACTLY is 'inclusive theatre'? An everyday analogy might be made with the original 'pure' aims of comprehensive education – equality of

Mary leading a Wednesday Group session.

Wednesday Group workshops at Vita et Pax.
Top left and far right: Rehearsals at All Saints' church hall.

RIGHT
From left to right:
Mark Goodhew,
Catriona McDougall,
Anne McGoohan,
Michael Williams,
Judi Dench and
Malcolm Gorrie in a
publicity shot.

opportunity, regardless of socio-economic background, allowing children to fulfil themselves through sport, art, music and drama irrespective of their ability in more academic subjects. What Chickenshed was embarking on – two decades before the Special Educational Needs and Disability Act of 2001 required schools, colleges, universities and other educational establishments to make 'reasonable provisions' to ensure those with 'disabilities' or 'special needs' were afforded equality of opportunity – was really rather revolutionary. 'Excellence without exclusion' is how Chickenshed sums it up.

Chickenshed was, from the very outset, open to everyone, but, like John at Cheviots, Jo, Mary and their colleagues aim to achieve a balance – racial, social, ability and disability, age – so that Chickenshed is a microcosm of society as a whole. 'We aim for a mixed group that's representative of society. We try to represent in each group – Children's Theatre, Youth Theatre and the Adult Theatre Workshop – what society is like,' says Jo. That means some people will have no problems, while others will simply *appear* as if they have no problems. And, as Dom Placid had suggested, shyness, privilege, exceptional brightness – all could make life difficult. Members are known by their names, not their disabilities.

If Chickenshed isn't a 'do-gooding place', neither is it 'a namby-pamby stage school. We don't make you into

stars,' Jo continues. 'We don't audition, you just go on a list and join. *Everybody* has an ability – we find it.' Wherever that ability is ultimately deployed – on stage, backstage, front of house – everyone who is part of Chickenshed is a valued member of the community. 'We regard everyone who works, studies, learns or performs at Chickenshed as "us" whether you are a volunteer, a supporter, a student, or working in the administrative, artistic or technical areas of the company,' declares the first rule in an early 'House Style' document.

BY THE TIME CHICKENSHED entered its second decade, news of its innovative work had begun to reach a number of key figures who would have a catalytic effect on the company, eventually helping secure its future. From Chatsworth TV came Malcolm Heyworth, who filmed a production of *Genesis*, and from stage and screen came Pauline Collins and John Alderton and, most significantly, Judi Dench and Michael Williams. All of them were prepared to trek to the northern reaches of London to spend an evening sitting on uncomfortable chairs in chilly church halls, occasionally under a leaking roof.

The four actors had been introduced to Chickenshed by Sandy Gonzalez, whose children Tessa and

Sebastian (the latter – also known as Bassi – now a key member of the company) attended, later to be joined by her third child, Caroline. Once again, fate had played a hand. Part of a theatrical family (father Thomas Heathcote was a much-loved character actor), Sandy was casting around for a place where her children might acquire experience in drama and dance. She didn't want a stage school, and when she heard from other parents at St Mary's Hampstead about Chickenshed she thought it sounded 'wonderful, the right approach, the right ethos. So I got involved because they did and Sebastian let slip that I made costumes and masks.' The first show she worked on was *Alice* and soon Sandy was part of the costume-making team, the first of many roles, not all of them glamorous.

'My husband had gone out with Pauline Collins and her son was at school with Bassi, so I managed to get her involved. Then one day, waiting at school for Bassi, I stepped back and into someone – and it was Judi Dench, who was waiting for her daughter,' Sandy explains. As it happened, the two women were

acquainted: as an up-and-coming actress, Judi had been a regular guest at family parties. 'We clicked through the children and became friends.' Naturally, Sandy introduced both Judi and Pauline and their husbands to Chickenshed and they were all happy to help out, professional commitments permitting. Pauline, determined that they look beyond north London, in turn introduced Chickenshed to the group that owned the Piccadilly Theatre, which led to the company's West End debut in June 1987 with *Ferris in Wonderland*.

Meanwhile, John Bull, finally persuaded to join as a volunteer and then seconded for two days a week, set about reorganising the board of trustees so that he and Mary and Jo, respectively the Theatre's artistic director and director of music, had greater decision-making power. 'There was no organisation, no administration and no money,' John recalls. 'I'd always raised money for Cheviots, so I knew what worked, though Chickenshed's needs were in a different league.' In 1986, with a modest fundraising evening at Jo's New Barnet wine bar, the Greedy

LEFT
John Alderton and Pauline Collins in the garden at their home with Chickenshed members.

INSET
Sandy Gonzalez at Vita et Pax.

Grape, Chickenshed was launched as a charitable trust. Judi came along.

It was John who realised that, with little or no money coming from grant-giving bodies, Chickenshed needed to generate its own income if it was to survive. Children's and Youth Theatre were identified as key areas of potential growth: projects would be set up with schools in Enfield and the adjoining boroughs of Barnet and Haringey which would take inclusive theatre into schools – Theatre in Inclusive Education (TIIE). The workshops, which would demonstrate that children from mainstream and special schools could work and play together, would be run by a small group of teen-

agers who were most committed to Chickenshed. They were to be called Schools Liaison Officer Borough, or SLOBs, and they would be modestly paid. Jo and Mary were still working for nothing.

Membership was growing, around 200 by the mid-1980s, but the company had been homeless since the death of Lady Elizabeth Byng and the loss of her chicken shed. From the very outset, Jo and Mary had dreamed of their own theatre and they never lost their faith, but as Chickenshed slogged from church hall to draughty church hall, it must have seemed a long way off. Vita et Pax, for all its difficulties, was at least a known quantity; others could be far more idiosyncratic.

At one, the parish priest was himself an aspiring writer who thought he knew better than Jo and Mary what was needed. Sometimes, they'd turn up with a group of kids to find a building locked, the caretaker gone AWOL, leaving them no alternative but to continue with an outdoor workshop. Occasionally, there'd be a double booking: one day they found themselves competing with a dog-grooming session.

'We wanted to create more and more productions – we were hiring in stages and lights – but there were so many obstacles that we couldn't attain the standards we knew were possible and we were getting more and more frustrated,' Jo recalls. 'So we decided we'd make a *really*

concerted effort to get either a piece of land or a disused building that we could call our own.' Sandy hosted a brainstorming lunch at her Muswell Hill home. Among those sitting round the table were Judi and Michael. Everyone agreed that they would simply have to ask anyone they knew who might possibly be able to help.

Now Jo and Mary met with the chief executive of Enfield, Brian McAndrew. He was 'charismatic, for-ward-thinking and very persuasive', according to John Bull, who'd already told him all about Chickenshed. In-deed, having increased John's secondment to five days a week, Brian would shortly grant him the favour of early retirement and a lump-sum pension, thus enabling his

ABOVE
Left: Old-time musical buskers led by Matthew Lyons (in striped shirt) as a young Chickenshed member; he is now head of membership.

Right: Jo and Mary with Judi Dench and Michael Williams.

full-time engagement with Chickenshed. Some twenty-five years on, Brian remembers that first encounter with 'two really formidable women – not intimidating, just enthusiastic and determined and full of ideas. *Irresistible*. You get lots of ideas brought to you when you're chief executive, but theirs seemed to me more than a bit different and I had a sense that if they were steering it, it would get there. They were so committed.'

They needed to be: asking for land was no trifling request. The chief executive talked to his directors, who naturally told him it couldn't be done: 'I said, "Come *on*, lads, it *can*! Let's put our heads, thoughts and energies round the problem." I started talking to local politicians, councillors. They were cautious at first, but I was trusted by both parties.'

Judi, meanwhile, phoned Lady Jane Rayne, a friend from the National Theatre, of which her husband, Lord Max Rayne, had been a long-serving chairman. Born in the East End into a Polish-Jewish family, Lord Rayne had joined his father's tailoring business before moving into property, gaining a reputation for closing complex deals. The fortune he had made was poured into various charities, mostly medicine and the arts, anonymously at first and later through the Rayne Foundation, which, at the time of his death in 2003, was giving away some £2 million annually.

Lady Rayne: 'Of course, we knew lots of actors and actresses, but Judi was a friend. She rang up one day and said she hoped that Max and I would be free to come and see this wonderful group in Whetstone – she mentioned a church hall. We'd had a terribly busy week and my heart sank. I didn't want to go out on a Sunday night and Max said, "Do we *have* to?" I said, "Well, Judi has asked, let's just pop in." Her recommendations were

"We don't audition,
you just go on a list and join.
Everybody has an ability.
We find it."

JO COLLINS

good, so we thought she wouldn't send us to some bum thing. We were so bowled over we stayed for hours.'

The date was 13 March 1988, All Saints' church hall, with Judi and Michael as hosts. 'An evening of bits and pieces, children doing little acts. We'd had no idea what to expect because Judi hadn't said much, other than that they were extraordinary. Mary made a speech and said they were desperate for funds – the rain was coming through the roof. It was a very hand-to-mouth existence and I could see they needed somewhere more substantial. I think around a hundred children performed that night, but already Chickenshed had 400 or 500 members and *loads* on the waiting list. We felt we could definitely do something. Max said absolutely, and on the way back in the car we talked about forming a group. Already people were trying to organise things, but they didn't have the contacts. We were fortunate in having contacts. We were so moved that we said we'd help as best we could to get a building,' Lady Rayne recalls.

Also in the audience that night was Brian McAndrew, who'd brought along the leaders of Enfield Council. His resolve further stiffened by what he'd seen, Brian now met with Lord Rayne to discuss how they might move this bold project forward. Already various options had been explored, with Broomfield House, set in the midst of the rolling greensward of Broomfield Park but long derelict following a fire, seeming for a time a real possibility. 'We were very excited – I was imagining staging *A Midsummer Night's Dream* out of doors,' Mary remembers with a laugh. Enfield spent £50,000 on a feasibility study, but English Heritage killed the project with its insistence that no changes be made to the building, effectively prohibiting its redevelopment as a theatre. Moreover, the local bowls club was refusing to budge – 'Enfield's head of Leisure and Arts said he'd never met a more militant group of people,' says Jo. Most upsettingly, there was a good deal of opposition to Chickenshed itself as local residents worried about their property values and expressed concern about 'a lot of mad people wandering around the park'. Today, thirty years after the catastrophic fire, sixteenth-century Broomfield House remains covered in scaffolding, despite having featured in the BBC TV series *Restoration*.

With Brian committed to finding land in the borough for Chickenshed's theatre, Lord Rayne – who came with his wife to another show, *Hal Blue*, the following month – accepted responsibility for building it. Lady Rayne, now president, vowed to raise the money through high-level fundraising galas and created a gala committee which included Sandy. She also hoped to get royal patronage which, as she had been a maid of honour

LEFT
The cast of *Hal Blue*, 1988.

Top, middle: The real Hal Blue, father of Wendy Shillinglaw (née Blue).

Rehearsal and publicity
shots for the gala,
Sadler's Wells, 1989.

Cast members of *Maid of Orleans*, 1989, including Ian Smith (top left), and Bridget Mangan as the Maid of Orleans.

RIGHT

Top: Chickenshed and Lissa Hermans at *Blue Peter*, recording 'I Am in Love with the World' with presenters John Leslie, Yvette Fielding and Diane-Louise Jordan.

Bottom: A performance of the song 'Let's Hear it Then the Noise'.

at the Queen's coronation, was far from being an impossible dream. For a start, her sister, Lady Annabel Goldsmith, was a great friend of the Princess of Wales.

To ensure everyone remained on side, Brian took key colleagues and councillors to Chickenshed's first major fundraising event, a gala at Sadler's Wells in December 1989, introduced by Pauline Collins and featuring Tom Conti. 'That enthused the leaders,' recalls Brian, who saw it as his task 'to pass on to the nay-sayers the sense of enthusiasm that had been passed to me. It was like passing a golden baton.' In fact, once the initial scepticism had been overcome, there was widespread support for a project that soon began to feel like a winner, just the sort of project to which elected officials, faced with 'thousands of ideas and limited resources', like to attach themselves. 'The mayoress of Enfield had been talking to Jo and Mary and she said "They told me you're a fairy." I said, "Don't you mean angel?" She said, "Well, I don't see any difference".' There was no doubt as to the role the bluff Yorkshireman would play, but Chickenshed had need of both.

While Brian and the Raynes worked behind the scenes, Chickenshed members, around 350 of them, were appearing in a variety of events on both local and national stages, and on television, with several appearances on *Blue Peter*. *Maid of Orleans*, an original

piece performed as part of Lloyd's Bank Young People's Challenge, was highly commended by judges and a performance was put on in the foyer of the National Theatre. That same month, July 1990, a thousand children from twenty-two London boroughs participated in an ambitious project at the Royal Albert Hall.

Anansi, a Caribbean-style musical, was an idea born of adversity. Mary was ill – her first tussle with cancer – and Jo and John Bull decided that a project that seized her imagination would do as much as any medication to restore her health. The Theatre in Integrated Education Project, only recently launched, was producing genuine results. 'Kids from mainstream school thought it was exciting if they went to a special school,' recalls Jo. '"Special" was very positive because it meant wonderful facilities.' Meanwhile, children from special schools got to work alongside their mainstream peers, and peer pressure, they knew, fostered development. The original idea had been 'one big performance' with two schools working together. Jo suggested they broaden it out, make it Enfield-wide. John wanted all of London, which meant there was only one possible venue: the Royal Albert Hall. The Sports and Arts Foundation stumped up the £20,000 deposit.

Wendy Shillinglaw, who had recently become the first paid member of staff, was tasked with calling schools and selling the idea at a time when most people hadn't yet heard of Chickenshed. Once schools were on board, the SLOBs were despatched to teach the songs and dances, leaving teachers with a pack to enable them to work on their own. A month later, the SLOBs would return to see how the kids were getting on and further tutor them as necessary. Not until the day before the performance, on 14 July 1990, did everyone come together for the first rehearsal. While *Anansi* – words written by Paul Morrall during a family holiday in Jamaica, music by Jo and Anthony – was less attention-grabbing than everyone had hoped, it had sold out, making a £2,000 profit after the £50,000 costs. And crucially it put Chickenshed on the education radar, with several teachers sufficiently interested to remain in touch. The desire for London-wide engagement would lead eventually to the establishment of some twenty Sheds, their staff trained by Chickenshed to work in their local communities, from Kensington and Chelsea to Hackney and Haringey.

Three months later, Chickenshed reprised *Anansi* at Sadler's Wells – its first Royal Gala – in the presence of Diana, Princess of Wales. It was Adrian Ward-Jackson, a director of the Royal Ballet, who had formally introduced her to Lady Rayne: 'I'd met her before, but not to talk to properly, and he whispered

Each participating school made a panel for the backdrop of *Anansi* at the Royal Albert Hall; these were sewn together in Mary's back garden.

Top: *Anansi* at the Royal Albert Hall, 1990.

Bottom: A music rehearsal; Adam Rees (age seven) joins the band.

Jo conducts the band and cast of 1,000 children. Francis Haines and Dave Carey are on keyboards.

Anansi, Royal Albert Hall.

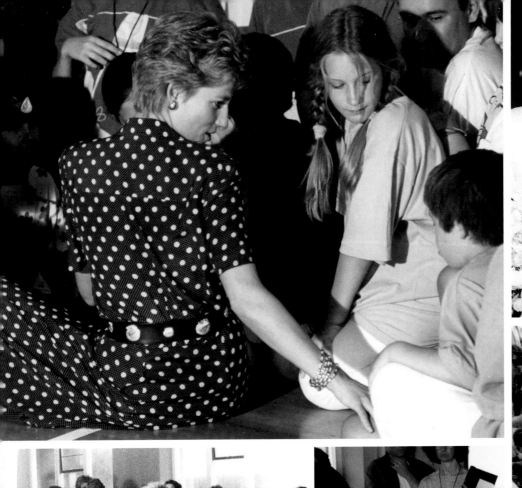

to me that she'd be very good for Chickenshed. I said she already had too many things on her plate, she'd never find time. And he said, "You can but ask. I've told her what I think, now it's up to you."' Lady Rayne found Princess Diana briefed and enthusiastic, and they agreed that, formal duties permitting, she would attend the autumn gala. Her diary secretary duly pencilled in the date: 17 October 1990.

By the time the day arrived, the Princess had privately agreed to be patron of Chickenshed, though the public announcement added to the evening's excitement, as well as to the news story. 'The show began with Lissa Hermans, then about nine, singing "God Save the Queen" in the way only Lissa can sing it, a sort of rocky way,' recalls Jo. 'Diana said later that the minute she heard it, she knew she'd get involved. She came backstage afterwards and spent ages meeting everyone, out of the public eye. The press just came to the show.'

Though she would drastically scale back her charity work at the close of 1993, Diana never did break the ties with Chickenshed, which remained one of her fifty 'special charities', remembered in her will, and her brief years as patron ensured that the goal of a purpose-built theatre was realised sooner rather than later. 'She loved the children, loved the dance, loved our choreography and she loved the inclusion,' Jo reflects. Something of an outsider in the royal family, even before the divorce, Diana empathised with members who, in circumstances beyond Chickenshed, were themselves outsiders, establishing a personal rapport with many.

Mary continues: 'We were lucky, we managed to keep her visits quite private. She even brought her children to a show and nobody knew about it. We kept it absolutely quiet and that really resonated with her because she felt very safe.' Diana even went so far as to appear in a fundraising video, filmed in Burford Hall, Palmers Green. 'She definitely opened doors. People would pay £500 or £5,000 to sit in the same row as her at a gala or to have drinks with her afterwards,' adds Jo. 'She *wanted* to be used. When she had the time, she would do anything for us.'

Chickenshed was clearly on the way, its administration now transferred from Mary's home to a small office in Enfield. Jo had joined Wendy and Mary on the staff, devoting herself to the company and gigging only occasionally, for 1991 was another busy year. Once again, Diana's presence at a Royal Gala, this time at the Empire Leicester Square, made headlines. Within days, journalist Matthew Norman's *Mail on Sunday* review of a ten-day season at The Place, a Central London run for *The Attraction*, 'launched us into another

LEFT
Diana, Princess of Wales, at Burford Hall, with Lady Rayne at the Dorchester Hotel, and at the Royal Gala performance of *Anansi* at Sadler's Wells.

The Attraction, The Place theatre, 1991.

Mary in rehearsal for *The Attraction*.

The Attraction.

ABOVE

Left: Mary enthusing about 'this wonderful land upon which our theatre will be built'.

Middle: Mary, Jo and John Bull with the Mayor of Enfield, Nadia Conway, as she plants a tree in Chickenshed's future garden.

Right: The shape of things to come.

sphere', says Jo. It was headlined 'Theatre with a message of joy', and began: 'Very, very rarely – perhaps, with luck, two or three times in a lifetime – we might see a piece of theatre so unusual, so astonishing, so profoundly moving that we come away feeling somehow different for having watched it.' Norman wrote about the unique cast: 'Each of them was splendid, each was on stage on merit rather than as an indulgence, and each was rapturously and infectiously happy and confident in their work.' And he implored readers to go and see the show, concluding, 'Go, because Chicken Shed [*sic*] is a magnificent ideal magnificently realised, as important and deserving a cause as you could find for

your money.' Researchers at BBC TV spotted the piece and Chickenshed was invited to appear live on *Wogan*, which left scarcely enough time to get across London in time for curtain-up. 'After that, tickets all sold out. We became very media-friendly,' recalls Jo, who handled ticket sales and publicity in her spare time.

MEANWHILE, BRIAN MCANDREW had written to all his staff: Chickenshed was to be found a home. It was Enfield's director of leisure who suggested that a scrubby area of land, popular with dog-walkers, at

the junction of Chase Side and Bramley Road, might fit the bill, which it did. However, there were concerns about the legalities, and tying up the various loose ends took time. 'If there had been a script for those early days, someone would have said get a grip on reality,' the former chief executive recalled two decades later, speaking of what he agrees is his proudest achievement. 'One of Jo and Mary's many gifts is that they create on- and offstage realities which were unimaginable to us ordinary folk.'

In January 1992, the news was official. Now all that was needed was the money. By today's standards, £1.3 million is a modest sum, but it was £300,000 more than

the budget set by Lord Rayne and it was agreed only after a good deal of haggling and redrawing of plans to bring the costs down. It was certainly a large sum for a company with few staff and which was completely dependent on the kindness of strangers. Moreover, it was for the shell only, and before the first stone could be laid, funding of £500,000 had to be in place. Renton Howard Wood Levin, whose projects had included the Warwick University Arts Centre and Senate and Shef-field's Crucible Theatre, had drawn up the designs following consultations with Chickenshed principals. While Lady Rayne continued to preside over the fund-raising, Lord Rayne, who had seen the National Theatre

ABOVE

Left: Jo pretending to take credit for it.

Middle: Sandy Gonzalez shows Diana, Princess of Wales, around the building site.

Right: Things are moving on apace.

LEFT
The fully equipped Chickenshed Theatre,
built in 1994, shown here in operation for
Pinocchio, 2001.

through to the completion, took charge of the building project. Princess Diana was an early visitor to the site. 'She put on her hard hat and clambered up the scaffolding to talk to the builders, who were of course thrilled.' Lady Rayne smiles at the memory. 'Without her, honestly, I don't think we'd have got the theatre.' A second phase, which included an opening up of the bar area, would be funded by the National Lottery.

By December 1994, the theatre was built, just in time for curtain-up on *The Night Before Christmas*. As the show went into final rehearsals, volunteers came in to paint the interior. The lighting rig was a gift, but the sound system was hired in for the occasion. 'One of our parents was an architect,' John Bull recalls, 'and he organised the painters, though we left areas unpainted to show people we still needed help.' The seats – donated by the Royal Festival Hall, where they had been excess to requirements when fitting out the choir stalls – were still being screwed down as the first members of the audience walked through the doors on 19 December

and all remember the 'satisfaction, relief and excitement' at the best possible Christmas present.

'*The Night Before Christmas*, in our own theatre with lights and everything … just an amazing day,' Jo recalls. 'We couldn't believe it. I don't believe it now when I walk in, when we're both sitting there today watching the performance. You do have to keep reminding yourself. Life is funny: you do stuff before you realise you've done it, and because you've done it in a haze of determination and tiredness and emotional strain, and blood, sweat and tears, you're almost anaesthetised to what it is you've achieved. And then you come out of the anaesthetic and you think, *We did it.*'

Sandy has vivid memories of the show's last night: '*Everyone* came on stage for the final number. Mary was in the centre, with what someone called her "crown of renaissance hair" and an emerald moiré top. She was standing there, arms outstretched and surrounded by the entire cast. The audience was in uproar. It was so beautiful, so emotional. I burst into tears.'

Lady Rayne and Councillor Graham Eustace with
Judi Dench as she signs the lease for the land.

The new Chickenshed.

Jo, Mary and John celebrate in the sunshine.

AMY AND JOHNNY CREIGHTON

FOR AMY and Johnny Creighton, Chickenshed was something of a surrogate family. Just three years apart, they joined when they were around ten and seven respectively – their mother, Sheila, wanted them to be involved with activities outside school and put their names on the waiting list. Then she found herself in hospital with Mary as they were both treated for cancer.

'They talked a lot, became friends,' recalls Johnny, who stayed less time with the Theatre than his sister but still feels great affection for it, always keeping in touch. He did just four shows, including *Anansi* and *Cinderella in Boots*, which he remembers with particular fondness because he got to know Jonny Morton, 'who was always making me laugh'. Both he and Amy were among the cast when Chickenshed participated in the VE Day celebrations in Hyde Park. Amy met Princess Diana, and remembers 'shaking hands with lots of heads of state'.

For both Amy and Johnny, this was their first experience of being around people with disability and Johnny feels that, without it, 'I could have had the negativity that some people have around disability. There is still discrimination, but everyone should be treated equally.' Amy, who now works as a teaching assistant, often with kids who are autistic or dyslexic,

---

"If anyone is in trouble Chickenshed go out of their way to help."

---

or who have behavioural problems, believes Chickenshed has made a genuine difference, proving that 'everyone can do something creative'.

Their mother did not recover and, tragically, their father died only a few years later when Amy and Johnny were still in their teens. Mary, remembers Amy, 'felt a level of responsibility towards us. She's very caring and, though she's always incredibly busy, she will make time for anyone she feels is in need. She'd come round to the house and try to help us. But we're not a unique case – it's a very caring and close-knit company and if anyone is in trouble they go out of their way to help in any way they can.' Mary is, Amy feels, 'the soul of Chickenshed. Private, quiet, calm.'

Johnny, having studied media, currently works in banking, but only to support the various creative projects he hopes can one day be his life: 'Chickenshed encouraged me to express myself and that gave me confidence.'

Adds Amy: 'It's fantastic the work they do, the outreach in schools, the productions on the road. Just the fact that the *building* is there and that's what it's devoted to, the fact that so many people have been able to study there … It definitely influenced me, and if I could find my way back there I would.'

LEFT *Clockwise from top left:* Johnny and Amy Creighton; Amy in *MGM*; in the cast of *A Christmas Carol*, 1997.

ARUN BLAIR-MANGAT

ARUN BLAIR-MANGAT is talking from Cardiff, midway through the tour of *Hairspray*, in which he's played Seaweed and Swing. He's twenty-one, and his CV states that he 'trained at the National Youth Music Theatre, Chickenshed Theatre Company and the Royal Academy of Dance'. It turns out he juggled all three while still at school, which he left with five A-Levels. He's currently studying history at LSE: 'I'm allowed to have a term out for *Hairspray*.' He's doing it, Arun explains, for the intellectual pleasure: 'I enjoy the classes and the structure and reading books by the lecturers. It's enriching – I'm not *just* involved in the theatre world. It makes me a more rounded person.'

Arun followed his two older brothers into Chickenshed when he was just five or six: 'I was really shy, but I couldn't get enough.' He made his stage debut in 1998, in *Cinderella in Boots*. 'I was just playing a villager, but I opened the show.' At nine he played the title role in *Anansi* and at thirteen he was thrown into *Globaleyes*: 'I was taught so many ways of moving my body – I was taught to dance with my face. That was my first experience of a physical theatre piece.' At the Queen Mother's centenary celebrations he played a leading role:

"Chickenshed's power is invested in all the people who pass through its doors."

'I sang a solo, alternating lines with Lissa Hermans – she's such a force.'

Arun recalls leading a group, aged around thirteen, and being paired with a boy who had learning difficulties. 'I remember being intrigued. No one ever explained – people were how they were, no labels, no differentiation,' he continues. 'There were always people in the group ready to help. I've never been part of a company that's so tuned in.' He's still friends with kids he worked with way back when, and still remembers the sign language he learned, teaching it now to others.

'I *loved* Chickenshed. It kept me on my toes, embraced my overactive imagination. It was a creative outlet for me,' Arun adds. He'd like to become a powerful enough voice that he too can change things. 'So many people know Chickenshed, they've already left a legacy. It's about spreading the message. They're putting people out in the world,' he observes. 'Their power and accomplishments are invested in all the people who pass through their doors.' He's delighted that Chickenshed is increasingly recognised as a place to train, though it's not a formal course like RADA's: 'They taught me so much. Chickenshed is a mindset.'

RIGHT Arun Blair-Mangat.

FAR RIGHT Arun in *Anansi*, 2001.

ACT 3
LESSONS IN LIFE

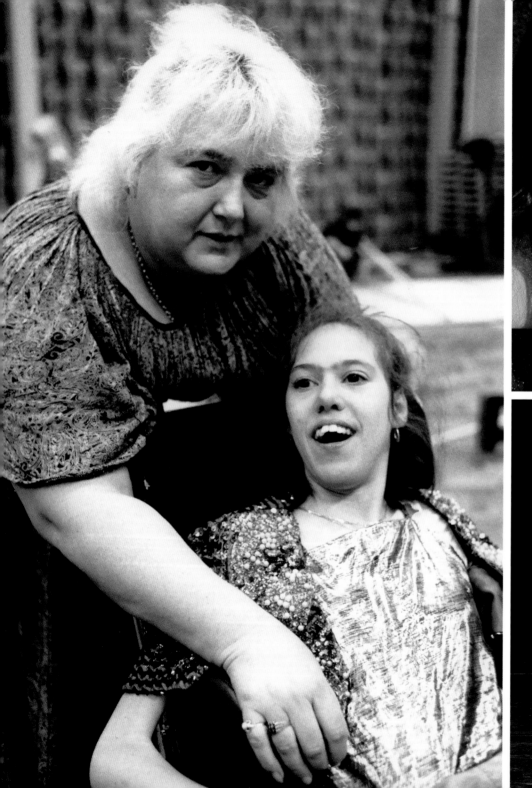

ON THE FACE OF IT, the ambition to build a theatre, shared almost from the outset of that 1974 youth-club meeting, was audacious beyond belief. Yet the unswerving commitment to the company that hatched in a scuffed 1930s church hall and took wing in a disused wartime chicken shed convinced others that the dream was not unattainable, and so it proved. After two decades as an itinerant company, Chickenshed finally had a home of its own – and with it, responsibilities.

Jo and Mary agree that 'it *was* crazy! We did it because we were driven by a vision. The motivation was the finished product, the final performance – that was always our massive carrot,' Jo reflects. 'You almost don't stop to look at what you're doing because you focus on the end picture.' So as New Year 1995 dawned, they and the company, which now comprised some 500 members, felt a surge of confidence: their self-

belief had been vindicated. The 'great family feeling' which had long defined Chickenshed was enhanced, boosting particularly the self-esteem of those with no family worth the name and no place to call home. Now everyone had a place to go, to belong. A place simply to *be*.

The year 1994 had ended on a high: there was a single, 'Have a Heart at Christmas', and an accompanying video; an appearance on BBC TV's annual *Children in Need* fundraiser; and, in the week before the Theatre opened, members of the company had joined Cliff Richard in a concert, 'Joy to the World', at the Royal Albert Hall. With the annual Christmas show behind them, it was time to embark on the first project of the New Year, *Paula's Story*, Mary's retelling of the story of Paula Rees, perhaps the most challenging – and challenged – member of Chickenshed, who had joined in 1988.

PREVIOUS PAGE
Warm-up in the Dance Studio.

LEFT
Clockwise from top left: Paula Rees with her mother, Jan; Rebecca Chapman with Paula Rees as the Snow Queen; Paula and Natsai Gurupira bound together in dance.

Born twenty-one years earlier with severe cerebral palsy, Paula had been written off by the doctors, who advised her parents to put her in a home, for she could never amount to anything. They refused, believing that their little girl had much to give, if only they could discover how. Today, she would be diagnosed with locked-in syndrome for, while Paula couldn't speak, she could understand and eventually, with the aid of first a word-board and later a head-pointer, she began to write lyrics, working with Jo and Paul Morrall, director of education, becoming Chickenshed's writer-in-residence. 'No one believed Paula could write the things she'd written,' says Jo, who freely acknowledges that 'she significantly changed us'. Paula's remarkable contribution captured the heart of Princess Diana, who wrote the foreword to a biography, *Paula's Story* by Shirley Flack, which provided the basis for the stage production.

Another member who 'educated us' was Lissa Hermans, labelled autistic and blind, who came via Cheviots. She didn't want to talk to anyone and it took weeks before she would even begin to engage,

weeks before Michelle Manzi, the member of the education team assigned to work with her, was allowed to touch her hand. Then, at the end of a workshop, she sat down at the piano … and played and sang what Jo had just played and sung, *exactly* as she had done it. 'That was the first time anyone realised she had this remarkable musical gift,' Jo recalls. Chickenshed had broken through, and Lissa's talent was immediately encouraged, not least through the gift by Casio of a keyboard. Stevie Wonder was persuaded to make the presentation backstage at Wembley: Lissa, reticent at first, was soon engaging in musical knockabout with the Motown star, also blind from birth, whose career had begun when he was still a child. He was so impressed that he also gave her his own keyboard. Many will have seen Lissa singing the national anthem at Wembley, at the Queen's Diamond Jubilee celebrations and at the closing ceremony of the London Paralympics. Today, she is still a member of Chickenshed, where she leads Tales from the Shed with the youngest members of the company.

LEFT
Francis Haines and Jo with Lissa Hermans, the young recording artist.

INSET
Liz Kitchen (right) enlists young percussionist Christian Morrall (left) and is joined by (middle, from left to right) Jo, Lissa Hermans and Anna Krantz.

Then there was Brendan Walsh, 'a very beautiful dancer' with Down's Syndrome. 'He just *feels* the music,' observes Mary. 'You look at him and wonder where it comes from.' Christine Niering, director of dance, who partnered him in Francis Haines' ballet *The King's Web*, believes that 'anyone who has experienced disadvantage or trauma will have something extra to give because it's all about release, finding a connection with something that's deeply, *deeply* painful. When you find that connection, when you bring it out theatrically, it's going to be extremely powerful.' Brendan, she sums up, 'dances with his *soul*'. Which was doubtless one reason that Princess Diana took such a shine to him. 'He wouldn't talk in long sentences, but she encouraged him and made him feel comfortable – on one occasion he asked her where her husband was!' Mary remembers.

Each and every member of Chickenshed learned that, in helping to discover and nurture skills and talents hidden deep within such colleagues as Paula, Lissa and Brendan, they learned more about them-selves, drawing on reserves and resources they didn't know they possessed. No one at Chicken-shed needed to conform. No one needed to be like everyone else to feel a part of the family. The only struggle, one in which everyone was engaged, was for excellence, a struggle requiring courage and an awareness of others, of their needs and idiosyncrasies. Excellence without exclusion.

IF SUCH A PHILOSOPHY was to be perpetuated, Chickenshed had to take it out into the world. While traditional drama schools might have offered a limited number of places for students with disabilities, those students were taught separately and, sadly, found work only when a script required a specific disability – although shockingly, even in the 1990s, it was not uncommon to find actors merely playing the role. Chickenshed wanted courses that were open to anyone, and, ensconced in its new home, it now had both the skills and the facilities to provide them.

LEFT
Dina Williams, key member of the dance team, with Bassi Gonzalez and Brendan Walsh.

INSET
Brendan, Christine Niering and Kieran Fay in *The King's Web*: the moment when the King finds the love within.

Moreover, an educational programme would provide a much-needed revenue stream to fund both the company and the Theatre itself, which of course needed regular staff – secretaries, janitors, cleaners and, soon enough, its own tech crew. Hiring in sound and lighting teams for the company's increasing number of shows made no sense, so Francis Haines, who ran his own studio from home, designed a system and trained a team to run it. Chickenshed had developed organically. Now it sought to close a virtuous circle, which enabled those who had grown up working with the company, some of whom had left to take degrees or train as teachers, to return and teach the next generation. At the same time, much as PhD students at a university tutor first years, so more experienced members of the company (and, soon, Chickenshed students) led the increasing number of Children's Theatre groups. By such means did skills cascade down the company, absorbed into the day-to-day, as well as being taught.

The Theatre in Inclusive Education programme launched by John Bull had proved a success, as innumerable head teachers who worked with Chickenshed would testify, and, by the time the company entered its third decade, it was remarkably self-sufficient. Like a magnet, it had drawn to it a number of practitioners, hooked in as volunteers, who would eventually be able to dedicate their professional lives to the Theatre. Even

those who didn't (like Francis) made themselves available when the call came. Somehow the skills and talents of the core group seemed always to be complementary. 'Like the Big Bang' is how education manager Jonny Morton sees its formation. 'This unique thing was created and then lots of individuals came along who made Chickenshed what it is today.'

ONE OF THEM was Paul Morrall, a drama and education graduate from Goldsmiths College who'd qualified as a teacher at Digby Stuart. As had Mary, with whom he now crossed paths at the primary school attended by her two children. 'It was a bit of a sink school, not providing much either during or after school for the kids,' Paul remembers, 'and Mary being Mary got cross with the fact that the school experience wasn't what she wanted it to be. So I came along, the innocent probationary teacher, and started up all sorts of drama clubs, football, netball … We got the girls playing football and the boys playing netball, caused chaos in the curriculum very quickly.'

It was the early 1980s, and Mary told Paul about Chickenshed. As Paul had grown up with a severely autistic older brother, what she said immediately resonated. His mother, very radically for the 1950s when autism wasn't yet properly defined, had fought for

Philip to go to school with his brothers, even though he hadn't spoken since he was two. 'The pressure in those days was to institutionalise him and she refused, going entirely the other way. So I grew up thinking that education needed a holistic approach with far more inclusivity than we had been exposed to,' says Paul. At the time he met Mary, Paul was looking for things that Philip, by then in his late twenties, could do 'that weren't so marginalised as to be awful'.

Naturally, Philip came to Chickenshed and, among other things, took part in *Love of Seven Dolls* at the Piccadilly Theatre. 'Philip, myself and a third person played different facets of the puppet master. It changed Philip, who became much more used to being with a wider range of people.' He is no longer a member, but the experience seems to have contributed to his ability to support his octogenarian mother, who now has Alzheimer's. Their relationship is 'so intricate … In his own way he has recognised that Mum's condition is progressive. He still doesn't talk much, but he realises that being with her and sitting closer than perhaps he used to *does* help. It's one of those beautiful links that social services don't understand,' Paul continues. It's not unreasonable to suppose that Philip's experience with Chickenshed unlocked something deep within him.

As for Paul, he started out helping with the Children's Theatre and gradually became more immersed,

not least with the TIIE outreach programme, putting in time during evenings and weekends as his own family grew: 'I wanted to work full-time for Chickenshed, but I had to wait fifteen, sixteen years. I enjoyed school, enjoyed teaching, and I worked in mainstream and special schools across the age range. I got to head stage eventually, though part of me was depressed by the promotion because it took me further away from Chickenshed being able to afford me.'

However, as the company took ownership of its new home, his ambition was realised. Jo and Mary had long believed that Chickenshed needed to work within the education system and Paul – who is today director of education and outreach – quickly opened up negotiations with Edexcel, Britain's largest awarding body for academic and vocational qualifications. 'We'd already had twenty years of developing programmes and we'd done quite a bit of informal, project-based work with Enfield College, achieving outcomes it wasn't able to get on its own,' he reflects.

To create a BTEC course from scratch, Jo and Mary turned to an old friend. Jelena Budimir had been around Chickenshed since her teens and had continued to help out during her student days at Guildhall and, later, as an Equity-card-carrying West End actor in such shows as *Stepping Out* and *Teechers*. Despite an unhappy time at school, she had been persuaded

by Carole McWha, her former drama teacher, by then working at a college in north-east London, to teach between acting gigs. In turn, Carole too had become involved with Chickenshed and the two women had co-written a musical, *Hal Blue*, based on the life of Wendy Shillinglaw's father, a variety entertainer.

Carole, who died in 2003, was 'a bit of a polymath, tremendously creative. She'd trained as an artist and then got into drama, and retrained once she'd had her kids,' remembers Jelena, on whom she clearly exerted a profound influence. 'She was an inspirational teacher who could talk to people on their level – a great communicator and a great influence.' A valuable combination of left and right brain, expansive vision and down-to-earth practicality, Carole understood the education system, knew what was required to structure a bona fide course, and so accepted the new Chickenshed post of programme manager. 'We investigated the different possibilities, A-Levels, NVQs, whatever else was around then, and we agreed that the BTEC had the necessary vocational framework for us to be able to make it accessible to a range of students. In the first year [1995] we had this wonderful group of twenty-four, aged sixteen to forty-nine. So diverse! It was tricky because Carole and I knew what was expected and what we had to prove – the course had to be really watertight. Everyone else was *yeah, we can make it work –*

which they could, but they weren't used to having to fit around a timetable.'

From the outset, results – in terms of both retention and achievement – were impressive and there were soon more applicants than places. Carole ran the BTEC for some five years before handing over to Paul in order to concentrate on the development of new education strands and trainee schemes that would enable

Chickenshed to build and retain a skills base that would support its theatrical work. Over the years, Jelena, while continuing to act, expanded her teaching and now also has responsibility for the creation of new work in the smaller Studio Theatre.

Middlesex University, which then had two campuses on Chickenshed's doorstep, had noted the Theatre's achievements, both in education and in the community, and awarded the two principals honorary doctorates, Mary in 1998, Jo in 2003. Having established a relationship, the university wanted to build on it and proposed a partnership. The first course they co-developed was a distance-learning post-graduate certificate in education (PGCE), which included a module on inclusivity in the performing arts, followed by an MA. 'That meant students were researching Chickenshed from afar, which was exciting,' says Paul, taking up the story. The next stage was an on-site course, a two-year foundation which developed into a BA in inclusive performance, all now linked in to what was going on in the Theatre itself. Today, Chickenshed is effectively a college campus with some 170 students permanently on site, taking both further and higher education courses and with the facilities to put into practice what they learn.

Paul continues: 'We developed twelve units covering every facet of Chickenshed's work – education, perfor-

mance, children's theatre – and we used it as a way to explain the theory and to put the theory into practice. We were writing the book as we were doing it and it took about three years. I wrote a good deal of it, and Mary the introductory module, but everyone contributed. I ensured that it worked as an educational package – translating a body of learning into something that can be an interactive learning package is quite tricky. It's layered on our work. We run and grant our own degrees, although the course is validated by Middlesex and subject to the same checks as any other course.'

The fact that many Chickenshed practitioners are not trained teachers is an advantage, he believes: 'That's part of my passion for inclusive education, in which all our staff are trained. Having gone through a very formal education training process myself, I know there's a lot you have to *un*learn. People have to be prepared to see things turned on their head. Whenever we go into schools, staff are amazed at the quality of our teaching – never mind the quality of performance, never mind the quality of support given to individuals. The quality of teaching is something that's always remarked upon.' Teaching is often in teams: for example, a combination of Jo's intuitive approach to singing, born of years of experience, might be counterpointed by input from the formally trained Dave Carey, associate director of music.

Chickenshed students rehearsing, performing and relaxing.

The focus is on practical theatre – students have to sing, dance, act, improvise – though there are also writing assignments. Paul emphasises that *X-Factor* fans are discouraged: 'We are not an agency or a stage school – indeed, the practices of some of those places are the very antithesis of what we do here.' Of the annual intake of thirty people, eight or nine might come from special-school backgrounds while a further half-dozen will have clung on in mainstream school. 'The rest come from ordinary backgrounds and some of them would get into any drama school anywhere, but they want to come here, which is great – we want to have that mix.

'We always push people, but some kids are terrified of putting anything down on paper for fear of making a mistake. They have wonderful thoughts in their heads, but they are inhibited from writing, so we encourage them to write freely and not worry about spelling and punctuation, which can come later. We tell them to get their thoughts down, to do what they can – and if they can't get any further but still have things to say we will sit with them and support them. Whatever is in someone's head, we want to get it out.' By definition, in an inclusive group not everyone's a high flyer: 'There'll be kids who struggle, but they learn from each other.' Too often, Paul suggests, conventional approaches to education restrict creativity. Those whose pace of work is restricted by a disability are allowed more time to complete their course: 'Many of our students wouldn't get a look-in for a proper qualification elsewhere – they'd have to do life skills.' Quite how much damage will be wrought by the high cost of tuition fees remains to be seen, but Chickenshed is looking for ways to ease the pain.

JONNY MORTON, Chickenshed education manager, hated his school, the local comprehensive, which his brothers and sister, Angela, had also attended. As a result he flunked pretty much everything, drifting through a series of dead-end jobs while working with Chickenshed, which he'd joined aged eight, following in the footsteps of Angela, 'one of the original Juniors'. In the 1980s, 'Thatcher's children' often felt alienated from society, much as many young people do today. The group 'gave young people a voice and created a real energy,' Jonny believes. 'Really close friendships developed and we did everything together. A lot of people were in relationships, they got married. That sense of ownership, of giving and being able to give, the creativity and freedom – that's what made Chickenshed what it is today. I don't think there's anywhere else like it.' While Angela preferred costume design to acting, going on to study art and design and then becoming a schoolteacher, Jonny studied

LEFT
Paul Morrall now ...

BELOW
... and (then) with Chickenshed's Juniors performing *Old Time Music Hall* at the Enfield Town Show, 1988.

RIGHT

Clockwise from top left: Jonny Morton; in rehearsal for Cinderella – 'Are you sure this harness is safe?!' – and as the wicked aunt in Sleeping Beauty – Dream On.

drama at Guildhall, finally having found something he loved. He graduated, got an agent, played in *The Rivals* at the Royal Exchange in Manchester and on the West End stage in *Lady Windermere's Fan* and *The Mousetrap* – and then came home to Chickenshed, in part because Paul said he'd be a good teacher. 'And I do *love* it.'

He's just finished seven weeks running around in falsies and high heels, playing the wicked aunt in the Christmas production of *Sleeping Beauty – Dream On* ('Baddies are always good parts to play'), and, like the rest of the company, he's enjoying a much-needed week off before term begins and he will once again teach drama improvisation and historical context in the performing arts. At Chickenshed, no one is paid merely to act: 'It's a cliché, but everyone has something to offer, so you create an environment where everyone feels comfortable and where they can contribute. You never give up on people.' Intriguingly, however, Jonny admits to having felt *un*comfortable with the 'anarchic and left-field' Wednesday Group, which changed the dynamic of Chickenshed and left him, as a teenager, unsure of his place, feeling deprived of his comfort blanket. He drifted away and watched from the outside as friends, including Louise Perry, now head of performance and his partner, reset the compass.

'At drama school you're taught about the art. Then you get back into the real world and it's not about art –

it's about bums on seats, and you look at the audience and you think, *What am I doing this for?* Jonny, as a new-minted drama graduate, realised that Chickenshed had real integrity: 'Of all the experiences I've had in performing arts, the most creative and the most satisfying work I've ever had is working here – and I've been lucky enough to work at some really good places.' The freedom and responsibility given to members 'motivates them and inspires creativity, enabling them to produce exciting theatre ... You've got the extremes of doing a great Christmas show, a family show, like *Sleeping Beauty*, and then you've got the flipside of our work with *Crime of the Century*, that's going out into the community and educating them.'

A warm and unpompous man who's watched a brother succumb to brutal multiple sclerosis, Jonny continues: 'I love performing, but it's a different love to working with people, seeing how you can change lives and how people's lives change you. We've got a connection.' His eyes fill up, not in any actorly way but with genuine emotion as he talks about what is clearly his vocation. 'There are people here from a world I would never have been part of,' he says, talking now not so much of those with disabilities but of kids who've never known the warmth of a real family and who've fallen in with a bad crowd, courted serious trouble. 'You genuinely care about the people and you commit something

of yourself to them, and that's exhausting. You're giving a lot – but you're also receiving. Because where else would I get the chance to work with the diverse group of people I work with here? Love and caring and compassion are embedded at Chickenshed, and that's an amazing thing. Humanity, coming together and sharing. People who would never mix with each other just being themselves, being open.'

DIRECTOR LOUISE PERRY'S first encounter with Chickenshed was as a fifteen-year-old, helping those with support needs at the Wednesday Group. She would not, she thinks, have joined a conventional drama group which required an audition, but, as someone already considering a career in teaching, she went along 'and sort of hid in the background'. She quickly understood the benefits of the approach and recalls that 'doing something for somebody else enabled me to do something for myself for which I maybe didn't have the confidence. I was just that little bit younger than the seventeen- and eighteen-year-olds who were really driving it and we were on the edge of moving towards what Chickenshed was going to become.' In other words, helping others to find ways to boost their self-esteem also helped her boost her own at a time when she 'didn't

feel valued or valuable' at the high-achieving school she was attending. 'I'd always been brought up with strong beliefs about making a positive impact – my mum, who was a really good teacher, had especially strong feelings about what we're here to do. If you wanted to work, unpaid, Mary and Jo allowed you to feel valuable and important – and we were.'

Watching Louise take rehearsals of *Sleeping Beauty*, with its cast of around 780, including four rotas each of youngsters in ensemble scenes, some with speaking parts, and the *Globaleyes* revival – the multimedia show staged by the students with members of the company – it's easy to imagine her as a teenager, leading members of the Wednesday Group, for though the approach has evolved it remains in essence the same: 'You lead from the front and you have to say things in two or three different ways to meet the remit of the group. It's then down to individuals leading the smaller groups to interpret that. Everyone's ideas are listened to and the final show reflects every individual view. Our shows have always had lots of people in them and a style of group presentation which isn't always about the minutiae of a scene or the lines, but more about a *feeling*.'

Always a reluctant performer (though she was persuaded to take a lead in *Paula's Story*), Louise left school to work at Chickenshed just as the Theatre opened. Having decided against university ('I was a bit stroppy

"Everyone
has something to offer.
You never give up
on people."
JONNY MORTON

and wanted to slightly ruin the school's statistics!'), she eventually accepted a place at Middlesex to study education and sociology, but deferred it as long as possible. When eventually she enrolled, she still spent more time at the Theatre than at uni but agrees that acquiring a solid grounding in the theory of education and how it should be applied gave her the confidence to challenge long-held beliefs. Working with Paul and Mary, she developed education programmes that combined the didactic with the experiential, formalising a Chickenshed theory derived from years of working at the Theatre.

'We were getting to the stage where we didn't want to be seen as hippy or separate – we wanted to be *accepted*,' Louise reflects. 'There's a theory behind what we do here, a very strong and defined theory, evolved from scratch from hours and hours of talking and meetings and practical work; of analysing and self-evaluation; of taking stuff apart and challenging it; changing the way you think; not accepting things but asking *what if it wasn't like that*? It wasn't easy for anybody.' Settled into their bespoke Theatre, the Chickenshedders, far from feeling grateful, felt 'militant. This is who we are! *Take us seriously!*'

With the ink on her BA certificate scarcely dry, Louise returned to Chickenshed. Hired as a project worker and charged with development of the Children's and Youth Theatres and the increasingly important

outreach programmes, she worked with Mary, supporting her on projects and, soon, leading: 'Mary has always been clear that the success of our work relies on the succession. For her it was never about holding on. Even as teenagers, we were empowered to make decisions, which were supported. Mary and Jo listened to us because they understood that their opinions had been tainted by experience. They hadn't had the luxury of being able to work in a group and make things happen – they had to ask *us* what was needed, which is what *we* do now with Youth Theatre members.' Ask Louise or any member of the company exactly who does what, who wrote which scene or which song, and it's clear that the creative process is entirely collaborative: 'I've always worked as part of a creative team. The lines get really blurred as to who's doing what – you don't "own" areas of the production. That means you have to have a really good sense of what your skills are and how they're developing, so you know when to defer to someone else. It's not always easy. Nothing here should reflect your own individual ego. The ego is *pooled*.'

Directing a cast ranging in age from seven to fifty-seven, each of whom is in a particular role, requires skill and patience. Work on the Christmas show begins in March when Louise sits down with the three members of Children's Theatre staff: 'We go through every name and discuss the positive reasons why each person needs

Clockwise from left: Louise Perry, head of performance at Chickenshed; Louise and Patrick Terecans pose for a photo shoot; Louise and David Rubin in a scene from *Paula's Story,* 1994, at the Criterion Theatre.

RIGHT
Clockwise from top left:
Louise Perry directing
Jonny Morton for
Sleeping Beauty –
Dream On; Louise and
Christine Niering leading
a workshop; Charlotte
Moulton-Thomas
teaches signing for use
in performances.

to be in a particular group. By the end of it, we've got people in a group for the *right* reasons, not because they *can't* do something.' When shows are written, it is with cast members in mind. Experience has demonstrated that 'there is no correlation' between (say) someone who has Down's or Asperger's and their ability to learn their part or take direction. A bright kid with all life's advantages can find it difficult to concentrate and take account of those with whom he or she is sharing the stage.

Louise and Jonny have each spent more than two-thirds of their life in and around Chickenshed and their own children have been born into the company. Despite the commitment given to it by their parents (weekends spent in the Theatre, rather than in the park, when showtime approaches), the girls feel 'really lucky' to have Chickenshed in their lives. 'They get loads out of it, which as a parent I would fight for, which is why I'm so passionate about the rights of *every* child,' Louise says. Ellie and Tilly have no special needs, yet there are times when they, like all children, need a touch of 'additional' support and Louise has no doubt that being a part of Chickenshed is as life-changing for them as it is for those whom society would marginalise: 'They get an experience here they just couldn't get anywhere else and they go to a really mixed school which we might not otherwise have had the confidence to send them to.

As parents, you're always told you should fight for your children to go to a particular school, that if they're not in selective education you're not giving them a good enough chance.' Those who are not selected are, by definition, excluded. Selection means a chance of excellence for the few and not the many, excellence for those whose parents may have the loudest voices and the deepest pockets – sometimes at great personal cost to the child, as Chickenshed has learned from some of its more 'privileged' members.

'I learned how to achieve in an environment that wasn't representative of society,' Louise concludes, thinking back to her own school days. 'When I left, I had to learn to achieve again, because you can't throw somebody out of that and expect them to have the confidence to do what they did in a segregated environment. My children are growing up with an understanding of how society is made up and the responsibility they have to accommodate that. They don't make the judgements or have the fear that I had at that age because I wasn't allowed the opportunity to succeed as part of what is our society. At some time, your child has to get out there and cope with people who are different. It's the bigger picture we're trying to deal with. Life isn't just about lovely smiley people. It's about challenging things that are really difficult.'

BELINDA SHARER

BELINDA SHARER, known to all as Bindi, first came to Chickenshed twenty-four years ago – her mother, Wendy, had seen Jo and Mary on television with Jan Rees, mother of Paula: 'They talked about inclusivity and showed some of the beautiful work they did – and mentioned that it was in a local church hall. We found them and we didn't go away.'

Bindi, who was born healthy but contracted viral encephalitis as a baby, made her Chickenshed debut in *Maid of Orleans*. Naturally, her mother came to see her: 'I couldn't find her – she was out of her wheelchair!' Soon Wendy and Stuart (Belinda's father) had an even bigger surprise: 'We were at a gala – it was the Princess Diana days – and Bindi came on as a dancer, with David Rubin and Christine Niering … I never saw it, I was just crying. They found this ability in her. Christine was the one who discovered her.'

It was a transformational moment, Bindi able to work with friends to express herself artistically. Dancing in *The Attraction* in front of Princes William and Harry naturally gave her a special sense of achievement. Most remarkably, perhaps, she toured with the show, away from home and family, supported only by the company. A learning curve for all concerned and a great demonstration of love and trust.

'I am what I am,' says Bindi, quoting the words of the song – music excites her,

---

"When I dance, my body is free. I'm not trapped."

---

though she prefers it with a beat, which is not necessarily what she dances to. Her most celebrated dance, originally created with Sebastian Gonzalez, with whom she is best matched in height, is 'Perfect Woman', inspired by ironic words written by Paula. Asked how it felt to be lifted off the ground during the routine she and Bassi evolved together, Bindi replies that it was 'like a miracle'. She wasn't frightened and she's never fallen when dancing.

She describes the piece as 'a beautiful story about a girl and a boy who want to dance – another way to show people that having a disability doesn't stop you from doing what you love … When I dance, my body is free. I feel good in myself – I'm not trapped. I am able, in my own way.' On stage, dancing, 'I feel like somebody else.'

Bindi – who was turned away from a BTEC course at a local college because it couldn't accommodate her needs, but who was among Chickenshed's first graduates – feels she has grown with every production. Her ambition? 'To be included, to dance.'

Wendy, who is among Chickenshed's band of volunteers, believes that 'people out there should know there are no barriers. There's no such thing as *disability* – there's *less* ability. Disability is a horrible label.'

RIGHT Belinda Sharer performing 'Perfect Woman' and in rehearsal.

LOREN JACOBS

THE HARDEST role Loren Jacobs ever had to play was that of Mischa in '*as the mother of a brown boy …*': 'The role sat too comfortably with me. I never get nervous before a show, but every night I had an overwhelming sick feeling. I felt I was putting myself on the line. A lot of what Mischa went through was what I went through.'

Like Mischa, Loren is 'a brown boy'. Like Mischa, 'I made myself left out,' craving guidance and role models. 'My mum taught me good morals, but I was easily persuaded and led … I had a lot of friends who weren't angels and we used to wreak havoc on schools and break in – not to take anything, just to run amok.'

Hanging out with the local gang, 'the challenge was to have a rep but at the same time be clever. If people thought you were stupid, you were looked down on. I got really good grades.' Loren hoped to be a tennis pro, so he had no interest in drink or drugs. Though he never used it, he did carry a Swiss army knife. And while down the years he saw lots of friends getting into serious trouble, his only crime as a kid was to steal sweets and crisps. The second time, his mother

---

"I was looking for a way out where I didn't have to wear a mask – I could be myself."

---

found out and 'frogmarched me back to the shop'. He was cured.

It was his mother who finally persuaded Loren to check out Chickenshed. She'd been coming for years, bringing Loren's sister, who spent much of her childhood in and out of Great Ormond Street. 'I was a product of my environment and I was looking for a way out where I didn't have to wear a mask – I could be myself.' So he joined in 1994, and did work experience before going to college to study IT, though only because job ads showed that systems analysts could earn £50,000 plus a car. A gig at Goldman Sachs was his ultimate goal. 'Then I got propositioned by Chris and Paul to work at Chickenshed … That was my biggest crossroads.'

In the twenty years since, he's worked in Performance, Outreach and Education, taking *Crime of the Century* into schools and teaching kids who may one day stand at just such a crossroads: 'Being broke is much better than being rich and unhappy. I've put too much blood, sweat and tears into this place to end up in prison. It's my lifeline, through all my ups and downs, my endless roller-coaster life.'

LEFT Loren Jacobs performing at Chickenshed.

ACT 4
LET GO AND FLY

EACH YEAR, when the all-consuming Christmas show is over, Chickenshed enjoys a week's recess, though the staff seem never entirely to be off-duty. Then, just into the second half of January, work begins on the spring BTEC production, this year a revival of *Globaleyes*, first staged in 2002 with a cast of thirty-five and reprised in a two-week run at the Edinburgh Festival three years later. It's been extensively reworked – the evils of globalisation are every day more evident, new villains have sprung up – and the cast is now around 200, comprised of students plus members of the adult company and artistic staff. A high-energy multimedia show with few words, some mime and a great deal of quite extraordinary dance, painstakingly shaped in workshops under the appraising eye of Christine Niering, director of dance, working closely with dancers Sebastian Gonzalez, Loren Jacobs, Robin Shillinglaw, Mark Lees and

PREVIOUS PAGE
Crime of the Century
at the Edinburgh
Festival Fringe, 2009.

LEFT
Globaleyes, 2002.

RIGHT

Left: Rachel Yates, associate director, guides a student.

Top right: Dancers exploring the innovative use of fabric.

Bottom right: 'We dance with our hands.'

Dina Williams ('my right-hand guys'), it is an astonishing ensemble piece which would do credit to any commercial theatre. And it's all the more remarkable for having had only six weeks' rehearsal.

Christine is also the show's principal director, working with Jonny and Louise, for *Globaleyes* was very much her idea, prompted by a reading of Naomi Klein's *No Logo*. Published shortly after the first anti-globalisation protests in Seattle in 1999, the book revealed the price we all pay for corporate greed, not the least of which is the exploitation of children in some of the world's poorest countries. The financial crisis of 2008 pushed Klein's once-controversial treatise into the mainstream, but when Christine read it back in the summer of 2001 she immediately took it to heart.

She presented the idea to Dave Carey, the Theatre's associate director of music and director of creative development, and the pair spent six months talking, reading, thinking: how to translate Klein's political arguments from page to stage? They also met with Anita Roddick, Chickenshed supporter and Body Shop founder, who had long sought to demonstrate that a successful business could be run on ethical and moral principles. Gradually, ideas emerged which began to coalesce into a series of tableaux dealing with poverty, slave labour, climate change, war … man's inhumanity to man, which leads, in the concluding scenes, to a rec-

ognition of the need for what the Dalai Lama describes as 'the oneness of humanity' and the late Dr Martin Luther King as 'the beloved community'. Both phrases resonate with Chickenshed.

AS IT HAPPENS, CHRISTINE, who joined the company in the early 1980s as a teenager, spent a number of years living in 'a proper commune, one which is still going'. She admits that both she and her sister 'struggled' with aspects of it: 'I was around sixteen, cooking for twenty people once a week, sharing pretty much everything. I resented not having the lovely home in Hampstead Garden Suburb, as lots of my friends did, but my dad was quite bohemian and left of centre. He felt he had one life and he was going to live it, so we were very influenced by him and looking back now I can see there's a real synergy with the way Mary and Jo were creating theatre.'

Christine's role in Chickenshed developed in a not dissimilar way to Louise's. A number of her classmates were involved and she was 'very into dance, going to the local ballet school'. The company was in its peripatetic phase, schlepping from one shabby church hall to another, but had by then begun productions in local theatres. 'I absolutely loved performing and loved

Globaleyes, The Linbury Studio, Royal Opera House, 2002.

immediately the way that everyone's input was so crucial. It made you feel valued.' A key influence was Donaldine Lourensz, who taught with Mary: she was crucial in developing the dance aspects of the company and gave Christine 'a space to be creative'. That naturally led to her beginning to choreograph and to a part-time job with Chickenshed between school and university – Southampton, where she notionally studied English but spent most of her time in the student-union theatre.

In addition to ballet, Christine had trained in jazz and Greek dancing. 'I love music and it always makes me want to dance. So in those early days my role was to go on my own to the church hall – if it was raining there'd be puddles on the floor – and listen to the music and choreograph the characters according to Mary's theatrical brief. After school time, children would come and I'd teach – and that was the beginning of it all. My journey has been so interesting because now it's about using improvisation as a tool, about using their response to stimuli, whether it's the music or the text, the set or a prop. How they move, how they're inclined to respond – that informs my choreography. It's very organic and I love working that way.'

So Christine is not a choreographer in the conventional sense of teaching routines that can be learned by rote. It's rather more complicated than that, for both

her and the dancers. Watching her at work, in workshops such as with Nicholas Sanford, and in specific rehearsals, you see what a collaborative process it is. And of course she's rarely dealing just with dancers *per se*, but groups of people with a range of talents and abilities, and disabilities – with (as the overly PC would put it) 'the differently abled'.

'It totally depends on the needs of the production in conjunction with the needs of that particular cast what process we want that cast to go through. Do we want it to be workshop-based where we're shaping it as we go along? Or do we want something more structured, more conventional? It encompasses all of that, but it's different every time. With many of the productions I've worked on, they're shaped by the cast,' Christine says. Working with someone who is blind, for example, requires very tactile choreography that can be 'felt'.

For those who haven't seen Chickenshed perform, it's hard to imagine how someone with severe physical disabilities can dance at all. Yet, sitting in the auditorium, without prior knowledge of the cast, it's often quite surprisingly difficult to spot those for whom their appearance on stage represents a triumph of will. It's a challenge for both choreographer and dancers, surely? 'The challenge is to think how that individual is going to communicate through their body, maybe in

LEFT TOP
Christine with Robin Shillinglaw in *The King's Web,* 1997.

LEFT BOTTOM
Christine directing.

conjunction with someone else's body, and to be quite genuine about using that as an *inspiration* as opposed to a stumbling block,' Christine explains. 'If you take the cast as your starting point, whether it's three or ten, and if the beginning of that process is improvisation, it's a question of *how can we move together?* If I said to you the feeling is "fear", how are you going to move? Trust is absolutely crucial; trust and a desire to push yourself. Then, to actually realise that, your able-bodied dancer needs to move in a way they wouldn't be moving if they were working with a different kind of body. Each cast is a different process, and that's where the excitement is.'

She cites the example of 'Perfect Woman', a dance routine that partners Belinda Sharer with Sebastian, or sometimes Loren. Bindi, as she likes to be called, has severe cerebral palsy yet years at Chickenshed and workouts at home have given her 'killer arms', as Loren put it during a rehearsal for *Globaleyes*; she has amazing upper-body strength. 'There's a pool of dancers who are on the staff and Bassi [Sebastian] and Loren in particular have really long-standing relationships with Bindi. They know each other's bodies, and that matters. It's back to trust: it quickly becomes non-verbal. That intuitive, instinctive feeling of *I can push this far, but I'm not going to push any further*,' continues Christine. The audience is immediately drawn in, not simply because the performance is so unexpected but because Bindi's

arm movements are so balletic and striking. 'It pushes a few buttons theatrically because it's inevitably going to make people feel things, *not* out of pity but because of the challenge and effort required to be able to move as she does. That effort is really important in terms of the *power* of the moment, and it may be quite transformative for the audience.' And for Bindi? 'It makes me feel free, it stops me from feeling trapped in my body. Dancing takes my disabilities away.'

Trust is, of course, key to any shared artistic endeavour, as important for Darcey Bussell and Gary Avis at the Royal Ballet as for members of Chickenshed. But there are surely added imperatives when working with someone who has a disability? Christine talks about Charlotte Doe, who uses a wheelchair: 'She's desperate to move, desperate to engage. Her stretch is somewhat limited, so we went through a couple of sessions in which we tried to engage people with hand contact, which, with a student group, is quite a process in itself. You hold the hand of someone who is disabled: *Is it OK, will I hurt her?* That's all part of the learning. I suggested to Charlotte that we see how far we could go, and because she feels comfortable, and because the environment is safe and trusting, she's happy to go with that.' Christine reaches for an analogy from the school gym, a place that can be far from comfortable for many of us: 'It takes a great teacher to connect with every

"Dancing takes my disabilities away"

BELINDA SHARER

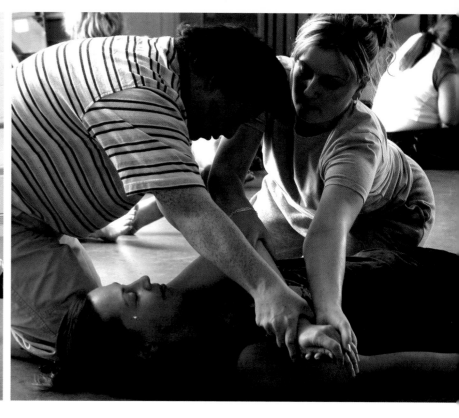

PREVIOUS PAGE
Belinda Sharer's
journey in dance …

ABOVE
… inspires others.

single child in a way they, as an individual, need. Here it's a given, and it does mean more time; more thinking about it, more observation, more communication. It's extra, and yet it's *not* extra, because it works. That's the way it should be.'

Everyone, of course, has bad days, but, with a group as diverse as Chickenshed, they may be more marked: 'You're going to get variables, but you know the person and you know what those variables are likely to be and you take it on board.' Years of experience have taught Christine and her colleagues to develop practices that ameliorate particular problems: 'For example, with

Bindi, over the years it's been a case of learning that there's a certain type of warm-up that will enable her to attain the stretch she needs, and if we don't do that before a show she won't reach it. Everyone needs to understand how to get their body ready to go on stage. Bindi always has cold feet, so when I used to dance and we were backstage together, we developed a specific warm-up. But you also need to work out if you're going to dance without shoes. Is it more considered here? Of *course*, but not in a way that's a hassle.'

However 'desperate' a person with disabilities might be to participate as fully as possible in Chickenshed's

work, to do so requires courage as well as trust. For most of us, it takes an enormous leap of imagination to appreciate what it would be like to be blind and on stage, never mind what it would take to leave a wheelchair behind in the dressing room. Christine agrees that she's witnessed some remarkable 'journeys', but she points out that fear and reticence are universal emotions: 'Every kid knows that the way we perform here is with the ethos that *this isn't about me – it's about everybody*. They genuinely have to understand and believe that *the audience may be watching me – but they can also see the person next to me*. By developing a relationship on

stage with that individual they're going to create something on stage that's really special and powerful.'

There's also 'an innate understanding' of the needs of younger kids, and responsibilities to them: 'Awareness of the needs of everybody is part of the training from a very young age. It could be my son Riley, who gets really nervous. It could be someone like Mika, who has Down's Syndrome, who's a bit younger than Riley. It could be Mika that helps Riley shake off his nerves. It's a two-way thing, constantly appreciating that one individual is not less than another.' Christine continues, with quiet intensity: 'We're *not* the same – it's not about

RIGHT
Dave Carey and Jo
in the studio: the early
days of Chickenshed's
technology!

being *equal*. It's about everybody having their own *oneness* and respecting each other. It's not less or more, just *different*. How do we explore it and understand it and appreciate the positivity of it?'

DAVE CAREY, Christine's collaborator on *Globaleyes* and much more besides, was a relative latecomer to Chickenshed. Unlike many of its leaders, he's not a local boy but hails from Hastings. Both parents were head teachers and both were very interested in music; indeed, his mother taught music, and later music education, and ran a choir and an early music group at the time when David Munrow was leading its revival. It was, Dave says, 'a musically chaotic upbringing', for his mother's passion for early music was equalled by his father's for jazz. Meanwhile, he and his brothers liked 'prog rock' at a time – the era of Jam and Madness – when it was deeply unfashionable.

'My father would take me to hear Sonny Rollins and my mother to hear Palestrina, or Bach's *Mass in B minor*,' remembers Dave. Not surprisingly, he learned piano, took all the grades, and the theory, learned all the concepts of harmony and counterpoint, and studied for A-Level music – but also discovered the saxophone. In 1983, he packed his sax and his bags and headed for Middlesex University, studying for a BA in the performing arts with music-making. An option afforded him a year in the States, which he spent at William Paterson University in New Jersey, where 'a fantastic jazz and big band leader taught me about orchestration and voicing in a way I hadn't learned before'. Probably not what his mother had in mind.

When it came time to find a job he found a gig selling ads in *Keyboard Player*, the usual foot-in-the-door: 'I wasn't very good at it, so I morphed on to the editorial side and starting doing interviews – Keith Emerson, Rick Wakeman, all heroes of mine, so it was great fun. Then I started reviewing keyboards and synthesisers. I thought that's where my career was, and it was a nice but tiny business. There wasn't a lot to do in the evenings so I got a job pulling pints in a bar that had live music, the Greedy Grape. The musicians who came rumbled that I played sax, so if it was a quiet night I'd get it out.' The owner didn't seem to mind and asked Dave if he'd play in a show in which she was involved.

The owner was Jo Collins, and the show *Gulliver*, which Chickenshed was staging at All Saints', Whetstone, in December 1987. Dave hadn't known what to expect but was immediately made welcome: 'I came from a background, jazz and classical, where there's a lot of hierarchy and a lot of snobbery and there's not always an easy route in. This was different – and everyone

seemed to think I was really good, so I felt appreciated and valued. That was the key thing that made me want to come back.'

From the get-go, he was intrigued by 'this mass of people', kids and adults, on stage together, working happily, and soon he was coming along to play the piano at rehearsals for dance warm-up: 'If anyone was learning a song, I'd mooch around and make myself useful. It carried on like that for a few years – the classic thing, popping in on Tuesdays between six and eight, then Tuesday *and* Wednesday, then Tuesday, Wednesday and *Thursday*. Gradually it went beyond a volunteering thing and became my social life – we'd all go off to the pub afterwards, or to someone's house. There were elements of family and there still are, though as we've all got older with children of our own we finish a show and go straight home to bed!'

Dave remembers the evening Judi Dench and Michael Williams bought the Raynes to All Saints', when Chickenshed sang a new song, 'A Place of Our Own', but he always thought it was a bit of a pipe dream: 'Then, out of the earth grew this extraordinary building. I played in the first Christmas show here – I was still doing the day job and still playing in a rock 'n' roll band trying to become a pop star. Then Jo said they were going to take on some full-time staff and I asked if they had anyone for music. They hadn't, and I said I

didn't know how to apply but that she should consider this an application. Jo said that's fine, start on 14 January. So I turned up on the Monday morning and on Tuesday we went out to a school and started doing what we'd been doing here.'

Inhibited somewhat by his formal background and training ('If I started improvising, my mother would tell me to stop mucking around'), Dave didn't yet compose. Then one day someone needed a few bars of instrumental music in a hurry and the dam burst: 'I have a very clear memory of a keyboard with a sequencer and I realised one night that I'd really got the bug, and I'd sit there composing on my coffee table in my little bedsit in Southgate above the bookies. Every time I got home from work, I'd be sitting composing till one in the morning. It was instant gratification.'

His first experience of close artistic collaboration was with Christine, and he found it rewarding. As a student, he had been fascinated by the partnership of dancer and choreographer Merce Cunningham with John Cage, the composer whose most celebrated composition remains *4'33"*, three 'movements' of silence, filled only by the chance occurrence of ambient sounds. Cunningham's own use of 'chance' was considered an abrogation of the choreographer's responsibility in the 1950s. Our perspective on it today is entirely different and there is a sense in which both Dave and Christine are also using 'chance' – partly out of necessity, given the diversity of Chickenshed – though to different ends: 'I'd write a piece of music, put it on CD and she would start choreographing it, and I really got into the idea that she would come back to me and say she needed another sixteen bars – or another eight counts of eight, as choreographers say. They won't count in fours.'

Together they have made something of a speciality out of what might be termed musical docudrama, taking as their themes pressing contemporary issues and creating from them theatre pieces which are simultaneously thought-provoking and entertaining, if sometimes harrowing. Undoubtedly, they represent Chickenshed's most enduring work. If *Globaleyes* took a vast political issue and made it personal, their next project took the intensely personal and made it political. The inspiration for '*as the mother of a brown boy ...*' was the death, during a police chase, of Mischa Niering. Christine's nephew was just nineteen, a bright boy, much loved, though his black father had found himself unable to cope with parenthood and had bailed out, leaving him with his white mother, Karen Niering. A sometime member of Chickenshed, Mischa *felt* excluded at school, with no 'brothers' to identify with, before he was *actually* excluded. Then, as the lyrics put it, 'you started to exclude yourself' and he fell in with a bad crowd.

In the weeks and months after his death, it became clear that Mischa's tragic story needed telling, and Christine and Dave began developing it during the inquest, with Karen's blessing and support. Until the last, they had no idea what to call it – then Christine remembered how Karen used to describe herself 'as the mother of a brown boy'. The issue of mixed race, and why mixed-race kids – a fast-expanding demographic – are inevitably referred to as black, was close to home. 'We knew it would be controversial, and the *Voice* had a problem with it. But other groups applauded us for identifying the brown children,' Christine says. A powerful and brave piece of stagecraft driven by a mother's loss and pain, the work seeks to understand rather than blame – and to celebrate the all-too-short life of 'a beautiful brown boy'. Workshop performances took place in the Theatre's Rayne Auditorium in May 2007 before its opening in Edinburgh, where members of the audience often sat in silence long after the applause had faded.

Crime of the Century, another documentary-led multimedia show, occupies similar terrain. An exploration of the issues around knife crime, its sad inspiration was the death, in 2008, of fourteen-year-old Shaquille Smith, the youngest child to die in Britain as a result of knife crime. 'Chris and I interviewed convicted gang members, a convicted killer, victims, police, surgeons, and we started building this story. We set out to create a

piece of theatre. It's very soundtrack-led – we recorded people and then I built a soundtrack around their actual voices. It's a patchwork quilt of sound samples that became a story and on top of it we added rap and poetry,' explains Dave. What one critic called 'a raw, passionate lament for fallen youth' debuted in summer 2009 at the Edinburgh Fringe and toured the following year. It is now a key plank in Chickenshed's education outreach programme, led by Paul Morrall. Members of the company go into a school and spend a week workshopping the piece with pupils, helping them create their own performance around which teachers lead discussions on bullying, gangs and knife crime.

THE WORK CREATED BY Chickenshed tends to be of shared ownership, yet there's no mistaking the unique imprimatur of the shows created by Christine and Dave. Each is edgy, not self-consciously so but in the sense that each takes its audience *to* the edge, discomfiting it, tackling profoundly uncomfortable issues (breast cancer in *Slender Threads* and domestic abuse in *Survivors*, a forthcoming production) and uncomfortable questions about society as a whole (*Globaleyes*, '*as the mother of a brown boy …*', *Crime of the Century*).

Each has broken artistic taboos and each deals with actual or perceived exclusion, Chickenshed's *raison d'être*. The success of *Globaleyes* gave the Theatre the confidence to push boundaries, but the impetus is passion, theirs and the company's. 'It seems to fit Chickenshed,' Dave suggests. 'We felt that if you put our diverse company on stage talking about an issue then it had an extra layer on top of it. We can bring an issue to the fore in a way that a "traditional" cast couldn't. It's just seems to be a natural fit.'

The fit of Dave with Christine likewise. Their partnership is, they agree, symbiotic – which is not to say they don't each work successfully with other partners. 'But I know where I am in this relationship,' Dave says. 'I know I can ring her at ten at night and say something's not working, and she can ring me. There's a respect for what the other is doing, an innate trust.' For her part, Christine – for whom music is always the starting point – can express half-formed thoughts and ideas to Dave and be confident that he will 'get it. Sometimes we try something and it's not right – and we both know instinctively.' She will often leave the recording studio for the dance studio with a CD of new music, trying it out immediately. 'Then she might come back and say that it needs to get bigger quicker, or that it needs to explode at a certain point and I'll go back to my keyboard and try to get the moment she's looking for. There's a huge amount of back and forth.' Christine acknowledges that working with Dave ('yin and yang') and with Louise, has taught her 'not to be too earnest, not to over-emote'.

Recorded dialogue, including speeches, is a crucial element in the soundscapes Dave creates for their shared endeavours, and, while once again they are on the same wavelength, Christine will often give him a list of quotes and ideas. The speech Senator Robert Kennedy gave in the aftermath of Dr Martin Luther King's assassination was in both their minds as they worked on *Globaleyes*, but then Dave had the idea of counterpointing it with 'When I Am Laid in Earth' (also known as 'Dido's Lament', from Purcell's opera *Dido and Aeneas*) which in turn prompted Christine to create a scene in which the singer carried a child. Designer Graham Hollick topped it off with a procession of shadows walking across the back of a stage.

Thus do shows evolve, through rehearsals and workshops – and over endless curries, often shared with Graham, who has a great deal of creative input. 'With *Globaleyes* we must have spent six months in various Indian restaurants just talking – about issues, about ideas; pushing it, pulling it. We knew we were going to take the audience on a journey, so it was a question of clarifying what that journey was going to be,' Dave explains. 'I find that exciting. I get frustrated with people who

"Come and see these beautiful human beings. Each has a right to take their place on stage, to express themselves."

CHRISTINE NIERING

RIGHT
Bassi Gonzalez, with
Belinda McGuirk as
Tinkerbell (top right)
and in *Cabaret* at
the Hard Rock Cafe
(bottom right).

want to nail it down in the first two hours of conversation. Ideas need space and if you try to force things they go wrong. I always have this mantra of trusting the process. Sometimes there's an element of serendipity, having the right conversation with the right person at the right time.' Adds Christine: 'It's not prescriptive, there's no formula. But when we've talked around it so much that we can't go any further, Dave is usually the one to say, "There's a shape here."'

WRITING REGULARLY FOR a specific company of performers was commonplace in centuries past, but it is unusual today. While it may occasionally mean limitations, it offers the opportunity to create parts which play to the strengths of known performers. When Mary asked Dave to write *Pinocchio*, chosen as the Christmas show of 2002, he quickly imagined the opening scene and song, an audacious *a cappella* melody: 'I knew Iain Whitmore could sing it unaccompanied and that it would work as a piece and I found it easy to write.' Like most of the Christmas shows, *Pinocchio* drew on a wide range of creative talents: Dave wrote the script, and Paul the lyrics, and Dave and Jo between them the music. 'It's quite organic,' Dave explains. 'As a rule, we shy away from crediting anyone – that's not how we choose

to work. You take a piece like "A Brighter Dream" in *Sleeping Beauty*: Jo wrote a piece with chords and piano; I reharmonised one element of it; she took it back and changed a bit of melody. I discovered that was how I liked to work.' However, the fingerprints of Dave, the formally trained musician, are all over something like 'Peekaboo', again from *Sleeping Beauty*, its inspiration Stephen Sondheim, and both musicians are to be found in the pit during productions, sometimes leading, other times being led.

What about the challenges of writing for such a range of ages and abilities? 'If we're looking at a piece of dance that will involve someone like Bindi, then it's much better to have something that goes across bars', and so is less 'regulated'. As to song: 'Peekaboo' – which lacks a tonal centre and moves through a number of complex chord changes leaving little for a singer without formal musical training to hang on to – was made more accessible by the introduction of speak-sing. Essentially, it's what nineteenth-century German composers referred to as *Sprechgesang*, a cousin of recitative and a device which composers as diverse as Sondheim and Bob Dylan have deployed in our own time, which enables them to better tell the story.

'We haven't got trained opera singers or West End singers here,' Dave continues. 'To deliver a musical to the standard of Maria Friedman takes years of training.'

So Chickenshed aims to make the best of what it has, which is not inconsiderable, producing 'the right material in the right environment. We train them within our capability singing-wise to where they need to be. If we find someone who we thought had a chance of walking onto the West End stage with proper training, we would tell them so.' At the first production of *Globaleyes,* the company included a young woman with perfect pitch, so Dave had her record 'Dido's Lament' in all twelve keys. 'Then I played around with it and distorted it to create a track, over the top of which she sang it in the original key.' Thus, music created with one particular cast in mind will often need some rewriting to accommodate another.

EVERY CHICKENSHED PRODUCTION represents a unique collision of skills and talents, each performance elements of chance and risk, courage and daring. 'Untethering what you'd define as your potential' is how Louise puts it. 'We all do whatever it is we need to do and within that we all do things we'd never have dreamed of doing. Isn't that amazing?' Christine no longer dances herself, fulfilled instead by her creative role. 'Learning to dance enables you to do other things, to grow in confidence and believe that you're a beautiful person. I know Bindi has been able to feel beautiful about herself.' Philip Constantinou, who has Down's, is 'an amazing dancer with an instinct for movement and a response to music that make him part of my choreographic team. I watch him move, watch him express himself – I'm wowed by him. Come and see these beautiful human beings, see what they can contribute. Each has a right to take their place on stage, a right to express themselves. Nobody should be denied an opportunity.'

Therapy is not a word you hear around Chickenshed, but the undoubted physiological and psychological benefits of music and of singing, on one level the simplest of human activities, is beyond doubt. 'From kids who are feeling unsettled through to real mental health issues, listening to music, learning songs, performing – I see the benefits all the time,' says Dave. 'What we're aiming for is always a good piece of theatre. But the by-product is undoubtedly therapy.'

EMMA CAMBRIDGE

'I'M HOPING to make it to the big time,' says Emma Cambridge, as she chats quietly amid the cacophony of a rehearsal break. 'There are so many things I could be up for.' Indeed, Emma, who proudly holds an Equity card, has played in *Casualty*, *EastEnders* and *Mo*, the biopic about the late Mo Mowlam, with Julie Walters.

'Emma desperately wants to do television,' explains Sue, who brought her daughter to Chickenshed twenty-two years ago and continues to make the two-hour round trip from Buckinghamshire most days – both women are now on the staff, Sue handling press and PR and Emma acting, assisting with Children's Theatre, participating in Outreach, working in the office and much besides.

Emma has Down's Syndrome and her mother, who talks candidly about not wanting her at first, battled to have her attend the local school; battled for her simply to be included. Friendship with local kids was never a problem, only the authorities: 'At five she could read better than anybody in class. She takes in *everything*

that's going on.' Sue was running a local club for children with disabilities plus family and friends, 'a happy group', when someone told her about Chickenshed.

'We went to see *Anansi*, which was an absolutely fantastic show. The music, the power, the action, the colour. Six months

---

"We all have different talents. There's more to us than people think."

---

later I went to see *The Attraction*, thinking it couldn't be as good. But I didn't want it to end and I went home and wrote to Chickenshed.' Mary replied suggesting Sue come to a workshop, so she pitched up with Emma and her two sisters, all of whom found a place to be themselves.

'I was a bit shy, but then someone came up to help me, because I was in the corner. I'd never done drama before,' Emma recalls. She was seven, and it was Robin

Shillinglaw and Jessica Willis, eleven and twelve, who sat patiently chatting, gently encouraging her. 'They were *so* beautiful with her,' adds Sue. Innate curiosity spurred Emma on and soon she was dancing in a Royal Gala and meeting Princess Diana: 'That got me out of my shyness. People had told me I couldn't do anything before I came here and I think I believed them.' Emma has proved them all wrong. In addition to acting, she took a BTEC, writing an essay about Walt Disney, 'one of my favourite animators. It was challenging, different.'

Emma is aware she has Down's and she's aware that it affects how others see her – they can't see past the label: 'On the inside, there's a normal girl who does normal things. We all have different talents and there's more to us than people think. You need to have a passion and you need to have complete commitment. And you have to go for it.'

RIGHT Emma Cambridge, and in performances.

NICHOLAS SANFORD

NICHOLAS SANFORD, a BTEC student with cerebral palsy, has already been on stage in *Sleeping Beauty*. Today he'll be dancing – out of his wheelchair.

'Nicholas really wants to do this – we wouldn't try it otherwise,' says Christine, as the music begins and a half-dozen students begin to improvise in front of the mirrored wall. If you didn't know, you couldn't tell at a glance that any member is less able than his co-dancers. But, close to, you notice that two legs, skinnier than the others, don't move of their own accord. You can also see that Nicholas has terrific upper-body strength. He looks relaxed as he is passed from one dancer to another. Back-to-back, head-to-head. Turned, twisted. Over, under. His legs lifted, gently, gracefully, their enabled movement integral to the choreography itself.

The music ends and Loren lifts Nicholas and seats him back in his wheelchair as the dancers break to deconstruct what they have just done. Christine has been filming as they worked: capturing the mo-ment is important, for there are no set routines. By definition, no two performances will be quite the same, but the participants must create a dance that they can *re*-create on stage each night. Just as a pianist talks of learning a concerto and getting it 'under their hands' – muscle memory as important as the intellectu-

---

"The chair is symbolically pushed away."

---

al process of learning the notes and the subtleties of their interpretation – these dancers must master their moves by re-membering what their own body does in relation to those of their fellow dancers.

They start over, this time with Nicholas still in his chair: one by one, each dancer grasps his right hand and spins him. If 'in-clusive' theatre had existed in the 1950s when Jerome Robbins was choreograph-ing *West Side Story*, this is what he'd have done. The movement is fast, exhilarat-ing. Then, with Robin a balletic counter-weight, standing on the back of his chair, Sebastian grasps Nicholas's hands and pulls him upright. The chair is symbolical-ly pushed away. Once again the young bodies collide and divide, rise and fall, making and breaking shapes in response to the music.

They all know each other, are familiar with the weight and feel of each other's bodies, the moves each is likely to make. They are all, literally, feeling their way. It's a process that requires the absolute trust of everyone involved, not least Nicho-las, eyes big and shining, visibly thrilled, whose life has been transformed. The hour has gone quickly and they have only scratched the surface of what's pos-sible. It's an almost biblical moment.

RIGHT Nicholas Sanford rehearsing for *Globaleyes*, 2013.

ACT 5
ALL YOU THAT MUST
TAKE A LEAP

IT'S MAY DAY, and while students enjoy lunch in the sun, Jo and Mary sit down with the creative team for the first discussion about the Christmas 2013 production. It's *The Night Before Christmas*: the show that christened the Theatre will be the show that takes the company into its fortieth year, a year that will celebrate the past, with highlights from the company's now extensive repertory, while looking to the future. Rehearsals won't begin until the autumn term, but everything must be in place before the summer recess, parts assigned, new music written. Mary and Louise will direct.

It seems extraordinary, not least to the founders, that four decades have passed since that church-hall meeting of minds and kindred spirits. During that time, tens of thousands of youngsters have passed through Chickenshed, taking what they have learned out into the world. For many the experience has been truly life-changing.

Take Graham Hollick, who became involved as a little boy when his family moved to the area. Frank, his father, had lived next door to Mary when they were both children – Mary's mother had been a major influence on him. In turn, Mary has been a key figure in Graham's life. Now a successful creative director with a portfolio of blue-chip international clients, he was 'nonconformist' as a child and, as a result, was put in the ESN group at school. 'It was very old-fashioned: if you didn't learn in the way everyone else learns you were separated out as someone who has learning difficulties,' he recalls. 'Mary's mum had been very supportive, telling my parents there was nothing to worry about.'

When the Ward and Hollick families moved to north London in the early 1970s, it was natural that Graham became involved in Chickenshed: 'I was prime material, even though I wasn't musical – no

RIGHT
*Clockwise from top left:
Graham Hollick; Rodger
Harries; Jonny Morton, in
make-up again; Emma
Gale, costume supervisor;
Greg Williams as an Ugly
Sister; Graham with Joy,
his mother, at work with a
women's group in Delhi.*

singing voice, no sense of rhythm. So quite often Mary would give me a special speaking part.' By the time he was a teenager, he was helping out backstage and soon became involved in production design. His mother, Joy, a couture dressmaker and pattern-cutter who had in fact made Mary's wedding dress, had also pitched in, designing the costumes for the *Rock* revival and for *Alice* – where her work had a profound influence on Angela Morton, sowing the seeds of *her* future career.

Graham was on his foundation year at Middlesex by the time the Wednesday Group began and 'absolutely loved' his engagement with 'the kids'. He continued to work with Chickenshed while studying textile design in Winchester, involving college friends in its first West End productions. These days, he makes time in his diary for two shows a year, spring and Christmas, and has been responsible for *Crime of the Century*, '*as the mother of a brown boy …*', *The Rite of Spring* and *Globaleyes*, working closely with Christine and Dave on the development of the latter. Graham brings 'the creative vision' but happily admits to lacking the technical drawing skills needed for set design and building.

'The scenery is really a frame,' he says. 'Costume is my thing and for Chickenshed costume is of greater importance – it has to work and to show people off to their best. Because the ethos is to give people confidence, you don't ever want to make someone wear something they feel awkward in.' Emma Gale and Rodger Harries, who run the wardrobe department (Joy still volunteers) are more familiar with the cast and work with Graham on the practicalities of dressing a performer who may use a wheelchair on stage, or a child requiring a quick change.

'If my family hadn't known Mary's family, my life would have been very different, so I'll always find a way of being involved with Chickenshed,' Graham responds when asked about the pressures of combining work with the Theatre with the needs of clients such as Nicole Farhi and Swarovski. 'I'm a product of Chickenshed so I believe passionately in it and I feel I use the philosophy in my working life. I love being able to nurture people, to take on students, to work as a team. I love the interaction and I think that's something I learned at Chickenshed. For me, it's important to do something that has a social value and where I earn my money *doesn't* have a social value at all. I wouldn't feel comfortable if I was just doing that. Chickenshed fulfils a need to give something back.'

But it's not just children whose lives have been enriched: often the engagement has been familial. Wendy Shillinglaw was just back from Saudi Arabia with two

Cratchits.

.see colours

'home made' from fabric
of house

Tinkerbell

SKETCH TO STAGE
Chickenshed costumes in action (far left) and, on this page, the sketches that inspired them.

Clockwise from top left:

The Cratchit Family, *A Christmas Carol,* 2007.

Tinkerbell, *Peter Pan,* 2004.

French Hen, *The Twelve Days of Christmas,* 2008.

BELOW
Wendy Shillinglaw, Grant Harrison and a young Caroline Gonzalez pose as royal guests for the 1986 National Children's Home concert at the Royal Albert Hall...

RIGHT
...and Wendy at work, now company secretary and font of all knowledge.

young boys and was going through a messy divorce when she ran into Jo and Mary. She'd turned up to audition for a part in *Peer Gynt*, which the Reverend Adrian Benjamin was staging beneath the leaky roof at All Saints', Whetstone, and in which some Chickenshed members were involved: 'I wanted to do something for me, rather than just be a wife and mother. It was a bit of fun, something to get me out of the house one night a week.' In no time at all, she was bringing her boys along and helping out at the Wednesday Group. Robin took to it immediately and is these days a key member of the company who has taken the Chickenshed philosophy to Ethiopia, where he and a few colleagues worked with the Adunga Dance Group and were themselves changed. His brother, David, 'who was always in trouble at school but who was never naughty at Chickenshed', found himself 'adopted' by two older boys, Michael Charalambous and Paul Hocker, schoolfriends who spent all their time drawing. 'David's now an international street artist and I don't think he'd be where he is now without Chickenshed. He found role models,' says Wendy, adding that she herself found self-belief and moral support among an extended family.

She, too, wanted to 'give back' and her volunteer time was spent creating a structure for what was still, in the mid-1980s, a notably *un*structured organisation. From typing letters and booking halls, which she would then transform into a theatre before frocking up to preside over front of house with Sandy Gonzalez, Wendy did it all, learning on the fly and eventually becoming the first paid member of staff – and the unofficial Chickenshed memory bank: 'When I see the audience raving over *Globaleyes*, I take great pride in knowing I've played a little part. It's now a well-oiled machine, but I *started* the machine and handed it over. To still be employed in a place I love is like winning the Lottery.'

At much the same time, Frances Thomas found her way to Chickenshed. A single mum with a seven-year-old son and no car, she found it easier to stick around and make herself useful while Daniel was enjoying his session: 'He loved it and wanted to be doing everything, but, as much as it was great for him, it was fantastic for me – gave me something social, evenings and weekends.' So she'd make tea, move chairs, take notes – and, eventually, 'do the book', that is, give the cues for the tech team, of which her son, by then twelve, was a part. Frances had found her vocation, going on to learn stage

"It's more than
just learning theatre skills.
It's philosophy."
JO COLLINS

ABOVE AND LEFT
Robin Shillinglaw, with Loren
Jacobs in *Pinocchio*, 2009 (top), in
rehearsal (left) and in silhouette,
dancing with Paula Rees (above).

management and, as production manager, bringing Chickenshed into its new home.

Daniel having flown the nest, Frances drifted away. A decade later, she was persuaded to apply for the post of theatre manager, which she took up in 2008. Maintenance, security, health and safety are part of her brief and also, ultimately, some 250 volunteers, including companies who give in kind. She loves the variety, and the students, all of whom take pride in their hard-won facilities: 'There's no graffiti, we don't get wilful damage. Sometimes there's a minor issue, but we deal with it carefully.' As for what Chickenshed has given Frances: 'It's very hard to put it into a couple of sentences, but it's given me confidence and social interaction and it's made me look at life differently.'

THE SENSE OF FAMILY, of community, of which so many Chickenshedders speak, could suggest to onlookers an overly cosy organisation that still has some growing up to do. There's probably some truth in the criticism, though it shouldn't be taken to mean that working for Chickenshed is a soft option: physically and emotionally, it's hard work. Yet any organisation that has grown organically needs, at some point, a corrective touch on the tiller, not least because right-brain

creatives rarely like to think in terms of 'business'. And with a turnover now of around £3.5 million, Chickenshed *is* a business.

There have been some incredibly hard times, but everyone kept the faith. Ten years ago it suddenly became clear to John Bull, then managing director, that a month or two down the line, the cost of salaries could not be met. Jo wrote a brief letter, hastily despatched to everyone on the mailing list, explaining that without an immediate tranche of cash, Chickenshed would go under: 'We had a *fantastic* response, everything from a crumpled £5 note from a lady in Brighton who'd seen us on TV to a cheque from Cliff Richard.' Some £250,000 was raised, around half from Cliff, 'reaffirmation that the parents, the people who'd been here as an audience, the great and the good, really believed in us'.

That was the closest call, and the inevitable result was a somewhat anxious tone to fundraising, insufficient recognition that trusts, corporations and individuals wanted different things in return and so needed different approaches. There's more confidence now, and the diversification of fundraising streams is proving successful, refined into short-, medium- and long-term. Good projects are still easily funded, but the days of big cash injections are gone and even those with money are stretched thin. Working with a new board,

and setting up a development council chaired by Josh Berger, UK president of Warner Bros., the aim is to raise cash – money from philanthropists who want nothing more than the association of their name with that of Chickenshed, in the the way it's done in the United States. Already strong, with a high recognition factor, Chickenshed wants to use its pioneering status to found an association of inclusive theatre, thus creating both a platform and a business arm that would enable it to organise conferences around the issues of inclusivity and to hire out its expertise to educationalists and to government.

WHAT CHICKENSHED has done well is to embed itself into the local community by responding to perceived needs, moves which sometimes spring from a recognition of a team member's own needs as they reach a new age and stage. A year or so ago, a Community Chorus was added to the offer. 'I suppose I have a vested interest,' jokes Jo, who, with Liz Kitchen and Francis Haines, directs the sessions, 'but I felt we needed to address the upper end of the age group.' There's no audition and no requirement to read music, and young as well as old are welcomed: 'The more mixed the better, though there are never enough men. It's very laid-back and relaxed and

they all come out smiling and happy.' The physiological benefits of taking in a whole chestful of air and opening the mouth to sing are well documented, but many people, worried that they have no voice to speak of, are embarrassed to try. Jo observes that there are always a few who start out basically miming and then get carried along by the fun and camaraderie: 'They think they can't sing, but by the end they've discovered they can. It's all about well-being and self-confidence.' The repertoire is light and varied and the plan now is to work towards an end-of-term performance.

The initiative comes under the banner of Adult Theatre Workshops, which include project-based courses aimed at those (often parents and volunteers) whose professional commitments make long-term engagement tricky. Led by Jelena Budimir, the Emerging Writers Workshop offers the opportunity to develop a script idea into a short piece which can be performed on the smaller Studio stage using the resources of both company and workshop members. 'We've always wanted to make space for people for whom performance isn't a routine part of their life,' explains Louise Perry. 'They have a right to belong and they're not patronised, and they've joined a cast of our students so they're working alongside a sixteen-year-old who joined three months before and they love the experience.' The initiative has brought in both new energy and new ideas, as nascent

Right: Workshop with
Pete Dowse, associate
director (on the left).

writers realise they have at their disposal a group of people who can, quite literally, act their age.

'It's all about creating for the stage, and we run writers' workshops throughout the year. We talk about the process of writing and we've had some really important work that's started as an idea and not as a script,' Louise continues. Indeed, *All I've Known* by Rachel Yates began as a ten-minute platform and progressed to full-scale performance in the Studio. Jelena runs the programme, with input from Dave Carey and Paul Morrall; Robin Shillinglaw works with them as a devisor and creator. 'It's all about finding the right pairings.'

Launched in 2013 following a pilot scheme, Young Creators is a professional development programme for those from fourteen to twenty-five years old, which effectively formalises what Chickenshed has been doing for some time. The aim is to provide training and work experience across a range of subjects, including children's and youth theatre direction, choreography, music technology, lighting and costume design – without the financial burdens usually associated with such study. There are three levels to each year-long course and every successful student leaves with a letter of recommendation.

The week-long Half-Term, Easter and Summer Sheds, launched originally as a way of providing an opening for those on the Chickenshed waiting list (children are registered at birth for one of the thirty places available

"Chickenshed
is a Utopia that
shows
how life can work
when you're all
together."
ANGELA MORTON

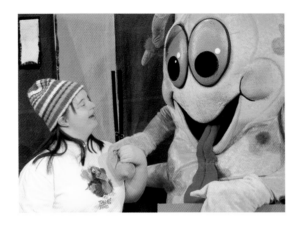

annually) have taken on a life of their own. Billed as 'Holiday Performance Workshops', they welcome kids from five to twelve for six hours a day, Monday to Friday, providing a Chickenshed experience in miniature. Five members of staff plus a support team work with eighty-five children using specially devised material which culminates in a show. Saturday Shed offers hour-long sessions of 'drama, dance, singing and story-making' across two age groups, while Tales from the Shed provides 'interactive theatre' for children from nought to seven.

Tales evolved thirteen years ago when Pete Dowse, another Chickenshed veteran, pointed out to his colleagues a gap in the Theatre's activities. Inspired by the Dadaists' 1920s injunction to 'tell your children your dreams', it encourages the children to share their dreams, their ideas, their flights of fancy in sessions which 'at their best, look at the cast and pairs, matches and stretches each one according to where they are at that moment'. A blend of classic theatre tradition and modern educational theory, Tales aims to turn every young participant into 'a spect-actor', a phrase coined by the late Brazilian Augusto Boal, named UNESCO World Theatre Ambassador, who, in different circumstances (amid the ghettos of Rio, the oppression of military dictatorship), aimed to transform audiences into participants in the theatrical experience. While Hamlet believed theatre to be a mirror which reflects our virtues and defects equally, Boal preferred to see it as a mirror into which one could reach in order to transform reality. Not a bad way of summing up Chickenshed itself.

AWAY FROM THE Theatre campus, the school projects are increasingly successful, a part of Paul Morrall's portfolio. He and his colleagues are always on the lookout for new combinations which demonstrate that inclusion works well in education: 'We like projects where we can take over the curriculum for a day or longer, opportunities to push the boundaries and show that performing arts is central to the curriculum.' Around a dozen members take *Crime of the Century* into schools and they are

'able to deliver at a very high level and in difficult situations', including young offenders' institutes.

At the opposite end of the scale, Chickenshed's corporate training programme offers an intelligent alternative to paintballing and other such activities. In 'a team-gelling experience' aimed at encouraging office-bound executives to 'come alive' and 'step outside their comfort zone', Paul works with Jonny Morton, members of the *Crime* team and students to create 'a bespoke' day which ends with a performance. Clients have included BT, Hilton and even Deustche Bank, who enjoyed it sufficiently to launch an in-house fund-raising initiative, an unexpected benefit of what is both a useful revenue stream and a brand-building exercise.

Further afield – much further afield, way beyond the projects with groups such as Cardboard Citizens, Place to Be and Young Minds – Chickenshed has fostered relationships across oceans and time zones. Back in 2002, members were invited by the charity CAFOD to set up an exchange visit with the Adunga Dance Company of Addis Ababa, originally a group of a hundred disadvantaged youngsters, which had already taken steps towards inclusive theatre via Adunga Potentials, a community group which included polio victims. Loren Jacobs and Robin Shillinglaw were among the six dancers who travelled out to work with

them, bringing back not only new techniques, including a unique way of 'wrapping' dancers together (which enabled Paula Rees and Belinda Sharer to dance) but also new friends, who in turn took back to Ethiopia ideas learned at Chickenshed – and a diploma from Middlesex University. Robin later returned to spend eight months with the company.

European Union funding enabled an exchange programme with Russia: Paul and Dave Carey led a small team to Moscow and St Petersburg, where they worked with like-minded people in mainstream schools and helped train practitioners in inclusive performing arts. 'Russia's attitude to disability is where Britain was in the 1940s – get the kids into massive homes, each of them numbered,' Dave reflects. 'The challenges were huge: we'd be given a space on the sixth floor and we'd have to carry wheelchairs up.' Tears were shed when twenty Russian kids stood in Red Square singing 'We Need Each Other', the unofficial Chickenshed anthem, its words by Paula Rees.

Engagement with China, where views on disability are similarly unevolved, is at a much earlier stage. 'Let's say we're creating networks,' Dave continues. 'We're also trying to forge relationships with companies in Malawi and Zimbabwe, and we've had approaches from Spain, the Ukraine and Australia. None of it is

ABOVE

Left: Rachel Yates shares movement ideas in Ethiopia.

Right: Belinda McGuirk, member of the artistic team, leads the children in a joyful dance in Ethiopia.

part of our core activity, but opportunities arise and we try to explore them.'

Such outreach serves to underscore the Chickenshed message: inclusivity is a human rights issue, yet even for many people in Britain, asserting those rights can be difficult. To help expedite the situation, the ShedLink Inclusive Theatre Training Programme was launched in 2000. The aim is to train community leaders in the Chickenshed creative method. The vision each takes back is necessarily different one from another, and no two of the nineteen UK Sheds (as they are called) are identical: what they share is the core value and philosophy. The first was Haringey Shed, the latest Hop Shed in Kent, which took around six months to set up; there are two in Russia. Chickenshed directors are always available for advice, but each Shed must raise sufficient funds to be self-sustaining. The exception, so far, is Chickenshed Kensington and Chelsea, the impetus for which came from trustee Christine Mason, who had always been passionate to see the Chickenshed philosophy alive in the borough. Based at the Chelsea Academy, it was established in 2011 as a branch of Chickenshed and is run by a small staff employed by Chickenshed itself, but raises its own funds under the direction of Christine. Already it is extending its reach into the community, working with children at the nearby Chelsea and Westminster Hospital.

FAR LEFT
ShedEvrika in St Petersburg, Russia.

LEFT
Woodshed (top) and East End Shed (bottom), with Michelle Collins, one of Chickenshed's great ambassadors.

Kensington and Chelsea, and the Sheds, which seem certain to grow in number, clearly provide the ideal foundation on which can be built Chickenshed's National Association of Inclusive Theatre, a future movement which would shape the development of inclusive theatre, ensuring that core values are upheld. It would enable the Theatre to build further links with community groups at local and national level. That would in turn support the creation of local networks of entrepreneurs, philanthropists and, of course, volunteers who could extend the reach of Chickenshed into cities and towns across Britain and, eventually, into the international community, solidifying programmes currently at the whims of Eurocrats. An American Friends of Chickenshed is already established, at present essentially a banking opportunity. But an off-Broadway production of *Globaleyes* is surely an attainable dream before Chickenshed's fiftieth.

CHICKENSHED HAS ALWAYS dreamed big and it has ambitions still to realise. But as it heads into its fifth decade of life it can look back with pride on what it has achieved. As a youth drama group which has evolved into a bona fide company, it has given untold pleasure to thousands of children and young adults who have

meanwhile learned that there is more that binds us together than separates us. While a surprising number have found what can only be described as their vocation at the Theatre, many thousands more have come to enjoy the experience, whether on stage or behind the scenes, and have taken what they have learned out into the world, applying the Chickenshed philosophy to their daily lives.

As Angela Morton puts it: 'Chickenshed helped me form fundamental beliefs about being a parent and being a teacher. When I decided to teach, at the age of thirty-nine, I had a very grounded idea of integration, of every child having a right. Everybody is equal, but everybody is different.' To those who would see the Theatre as little more than a bit of fun, a way of getting kids off the streets and away from the telly (both surely valid aims, in which it has clearly succeeded) and not deserving of proper funding, such comments go to the heart of why Chickenshed matters. 'I believe in it 110 per cent and would argue the case with anybody,' Angela continues. 'I would not hesitate to recommend it as a philosophy. It's a Utopia that shows how life can work when you're all together.'

These days, Chickenshed no longer struggles for recognition: its name is known by millions who have never crossed its portals. The Princess of Wales played a crucial role: without her very particular style of

Chickenshed Kensington and Chelsea.

Top, second from left: An invitation from Samantha Cameron
to No. 10 Downing Street.

RIGHT
'We put our heads
together and came up
with a great idea.'

PAGE 178
Globaleyes, 2013.

engagement, it would have taken a great deal longer to establish a home of their own. Diana, and the many actors and musicians who, given a whiff of the magic, went on to espouse the Chickenshed cause, ensured that it acquired a profile, with invitations to perform at national celebrations marking the fiftieth anniversary of VE Day and the Queen Mother's one hundredth birthday (arranged by Michael Parker), as well as on tour and on TV. Those events, some of them on the global stage, demonstrate both the reality and the value of what Chickenshed is creating – that it's no longer about good works, but about good work.

Forty years on, Britain is far more enlightened than it was and equality is enshrined in the law. No longer can those of us who are 'different' be discriminated against. 'Spastic', once the label applied to those with cerebral palsy and an oh-so-casual term of playground abuse, is a word rarely if ever heard. The joy of Chickenshed has always been that, within its walls, no one need feel different – yet life outside remains obstacle-strewn, metaphorically and otherwise, for those of us needing more help than others. When Friday night arrives, for example, Belinda Sharer – Bindi – can't just pop into the West End on an impromptu trip as her friends and colleagues can.

Over the same period, divisions in society at large have become more sharply defined. Money has enabled

people to leap over many a barrier, including those perceived as relating to class. Yet for those lacking lucre – the kids in tough areas, often from broken homes and condemned to go to sink schools – it is easier than ever to fall out of life's mainstream. To be *excluded*. These days, Chickenshed is a home away from home for many disaffected and disenfranchised youths who would otherwise slip through the net.

'Those who come here have their esteem raised,' says Louise Perry, whose own self-esteem was raised all those years ago and who is a key figure in Chickenshed's succession. 'We create in every individual the belief that the way we work is the right way and the most effective way – the most *beneficial* way. We *all* have a life that can be changed by this environment. Our life is limited if we haven't had this opportunity.

'Our strength in the future will come from our being representative of what we do. We need to get the structure right and the funding right in order to do what we do with the right resources and to the best of our ability, and to go into partnerships with other organisations. In terms of our education work, we've demonstrated what we can do and so the next thing is for us to be part of discussions with policy-makers. What we do can be seen as very practical and often people are shocked when they come here and realise there's a huge theory underpinning the practice.'

As Mary observed all those years ago, watching her mother teach, inclusivity, from the first day at school, is the way forward.

IN THE CHICKENSHED THEATRE foyer hangs a vast photo of the late Lord Rayne with his wife, Lady Jane. The inscription beneath reads: 'If you seek his memorial, look around you'. What you see, on a busy day, are scores of youngsters: happy, directed, busy with their lives but not too busy to look out for each other. At showtime, it's like any other theatre, the crush at the bar, the excitement as curtain-up approaches. Some memorial. Some adventure.

'We never thought about the reality,' Jo concludes. 'Had we known what it entailed, we probably wouldn't have done it. Mary and I spurred each other on, and then John came in with another set of skills and he spurred us *both* on. John Bull – he *was* a bull, it's the perfect name. We hired the Royal Albert Hall with no money. Ignorance allows you to do things you wouldn't otherwise do. I look back and I can see we sailed *so* close to the wind. The dangers, the perils. We were so *naïve*. But we knew a theatre would allow everyone to feel safe, hence the aspiration. There wasn't really a choice.'

This is what some members of our Children's Theatre have to say about Chickenshed …

"When I was experiencing bullying at school, Chickenshed was the only place I felt safe other than home."

"I love Chickenshed because I can express my opinions and views in ways I can't anywhere else."

"Chickenshed is one of the few places I feel I can truly be myself without anyone judging me. I'd be nothing without Chickenshed."

"Chickenshed is a place that is close to my heart. It feels like the only place I can really feel at home and be myself."

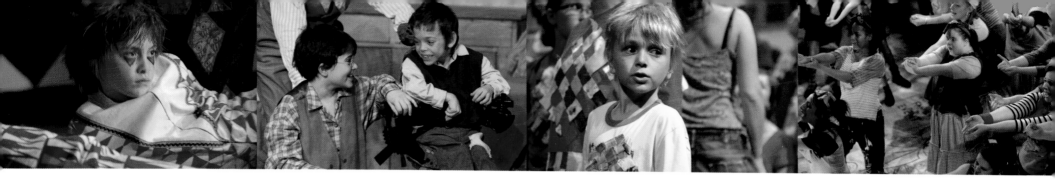

"I love Chickenshed because you make new friends and work together to create something you feel very much part of."

"Chickenshed is synonymous to me with inspiration. It's the one place where everyone is welcome and no one is ever turned away."

"I am so grateful for what they have done for me and I am looking forward to mine and Chickenshed's future."

"Chickenshed supports me through situations that can scar people for life."

Involvement

Chickenshed is a constant eye-opening experience from whatever angle you view it. Let yourself become involved. You will learn and develop in ways you might not have thought possible. We personally don't get things right all the time by any means but we can honestly say we try. This Company has succeeded since 1974 with others trying in the same way. Everyone should enjoy working here. Everyone.

CHICKENSHED HOUSE STYLE, FINAL RULE

APPENDICES

CHRONOLOGY OF SHOWS
1974-2013

1974
Chrysalis
Isaac

All shows are written or devised by company members.
Where shows have been inspired by the work of authors outside
Chickenshed, this has been acknowledged (page 203).

1975
Chrysalis

1976
Alice
Isaac (above)
Nativity According to
the Animals
Oh! What a Lovely War
Rock
Rock Nativity

1977
Alice
Chrysalis
If You're Glad, I'll Be Frank
Queens in Fantasy
Rock (below)

1978
Beggar (above)
Bugsy
Lord of the Flies
No Strings Attached
Rock

1979
Alice
Beggar
Bugsy
The Dot and the Line
No Strings Attached (below)
Red Riding Hood/Snow White/
Queens in Fantasy
Rock

1981
Alice's Adventures in Wonderland
Alice Through the Looking Glass *(below)*
Krypto Kid and the Amazing Egghead
Rock

1983
Charlie and the Chocolate Factory
Genesis
The Night Before Christmas
Peace by Peace
Pinocchio

1980
Benedict
Christmas Rapping
Laundry Girls
Stargaze
Tom

1982
Genesis
Strawberry Fields Forever

1984
Cinderella
Genesis
Old Time Music Hall
Ruth
Spring Show

1985
Bugsy
Christmas Rapping
Genesis *(below)*
Stepney Doo-Wap
The Wizard of Oz

1987
Bazaar and Rummage
Ferris in Wonderland
Gulliver
Journey to Jo'burg

1989
Cinderella
Gala
Maid of Orleans
The Treatment
Who Me?

1986
Christmas in the 20th Century
Molotov Cocktail
Outlaw
Read All About It
The Wizard of Oz *(above)*

1988
Anansi
Hal Blue
Love of Seven Dolls
This

1991
The Attraction
Best of Chickenshed
Dazey Chain
Faith, Hope and Charity
A Magical History Tour
Middle 8
Street Kids
Tunnel of Love

1993
The Beggar's Opera
Circus of Dreams
Life Crisis
Paula's Story
Signs of Dance

1990
Anansi
The Attraction
Hamlet
The King's Web
Maid of Orleans

1992
Anansi
Final Reel
The Lost Soul
The Night Before Christmas *(left)*
(Top right: Diana, Princess of Wales, meets the cast at The Place Theatre.)
Pericles
Rhythm of Life
Story Teller
What the Devil

1994
Bits and Pieces
Circus of Dreams
Final Reel
MGM (Making Great Movies)
The Night Before Christmas
Oh! What a Lovely War
Paula's Story
Pulse Twice Beat
The Rhythm Kids
Signs of Dance

1996
1984
Arthur, The Knight Before Christmas
Boubile
Magical History Tour
A Midsummer Night's Dream
Operation Pied Piper
To Be or Not to Be
An Unhealthy Business

1995
1984 • 2084
The Attraction
Flower Games
The Insect Play
The King's Web
(Brendan Walsh, right)
MGM
The Night Before
Christmas with Alice
Now Then • Paula's Story
Storyworld • Tell Tale
An Unhealthy Business

1997
The Ancient Mariner
A Christmas Carol
Darnaby's Space Race
The King's Web *(far right)*
Maskmaker
A Midsummer Night's Dream
Roller's Bouncy Day
Romeo and Juliet and
the Sonnets and Soliloquies
The Tempest
World Against World
Zero the Hero

1999
The Beggar's Opera
Darnaby's Space Race
The Dragon Show
In Darkness Remains
Interval • The King's Web
Light Comes Closer
Myths and Legends
Oriah Mountain Dreamer
Paula's Story
The Resistible Rise of Arturo Ui
Sleeping Beauty
State of Independence

2001
Anansi
Animal Farm
The Dragon
Extension 000
The Laughing Man
Pinocchio
(below, and far right top)
War Poets
Widows

1998
Anansi • Cinderella in Boots
Darnaby's Space Race
Land
Olaf Olsen and the
Champions of Who Wood
The Rite of Spring
*(above, performed on two
pianos by Dave Carey
and Francis Haines, with
Chickenshed's dancers in front;
and right, with Bassi Gonzalez
and Brendan Walsh)*
That Football Thing

2000
Blood Wedding
Brave New World
Extension 000
Greece – The Mythical
Oh! What a Lovely War
*(far right bottom, featuring corporals
Tommy Doyle and Katharine Woolfe)*
Paula's Story
Peter Pan
Romeo and Juliet
Tales from the Shed
That Football Thing 2

A Midsummer Night's Dream, 2002.

Romeo and Juliet, 2002.

2002

Blood Wedding

Globaleyes

A Midsummer Night's Dream

The Nutcracker and the Mouse King

Romeo and Juliet

Teechers

The Would Be Gentleman

2004

Alice on the Underground

On the Surface

Our Country's Good

Peter Pan *(right)*

Under Your Feet

2003

Alice on the Underground

The Caucasian Chalk Circle

The Insect Play

The Last Word

Love of Seven Dolls

The Night Before Christmas

Upon the Stones

2005

Alice's Adventures in Wonderland

Brer Rabbit

Globaleyes

Killing Me Softly

Lysistrata

Venue 32

Charlotte Bull (centre, back row), now director of Children's Theatre, as Mrs Cratchit in *The Night Before Christmas*, 2003.

Alice on the Underground, 2004.

Grimm Nights and Everafter Days, 2006.

A Christmas Carol, 2007.

2009

12 to 1

'as the mother of a brown boy ...'

The Attraction

Crime of the Century

Heads or Tales

In Watermelon Sugar (below)

My Life Through Your Eyes

The One and Only

The People's Happiness

(far right bottom)

Pinocchio

2007

'as the mother of a brown boy ...'

A Christmas Carol (below)

ME? Incognito

My Space or Yours?

Vanity Fair

Yard Gal

2006

Grimm Nights and
Everafter Days

How We Met

J's Son and the Argonuts

Virginia's Wolf

Who's Afraid of
Virginia's Sister?

2008

2020

'as the mother of a brown boy ...'

Avocado Sweets

Fairies' Tale

SeaChange (right,
and far right top)

The Shelter

The Twelve Days of Christmas

Yard Gal

The Twelve Days of Christmas, 2008.

Pinocchio, 2009.

2011
1984
Cinderella
Christmas Tales
Crime of the Century
Duty
Gameism
The King's Web
Mini Myths
The Rain That Washes
Shadowbox
Slender Threads
Story Tales

2013
All I've Known • Chao and the Chill
Christmas Tales • Crime of the Century
Evolution • Fairies' Tale
Globaleyes 2013
The Government Inspector
Into-net • Let the Sun Shine
Lord of the Flies • Lysistrata
Molecular Massy
The Night Before Christmas
Professor Hallux Alwie
The Rain That Washes
Sleep Perchance to Dream
Unsettled

2010
Badjelly's Bad Christmas
Come Follow Me
Crime of the Century
A Midsummer Night's Dream
Once There Were Monsters
Right Behind the Sofa
SeaChange
Sorry I Was Miles Away
Swaggerville
A Tale of One City
A Tales Midsummer Daydream

2012
Can't Pay, Won't Pay!
Christmas Tales
Crime of the Century
The Grandfathers
Olivia Twisted
The Rain That Washes *(above)*
The Red Shoes
Run, Brer Rabbit, Run
Shakespeare's Island
Sleeping Beauty – Dream On
Sunshine on a Rainy Day
These Four Walls

The following shows are based on the work of authors outside Chickenshed:

1984 (George Orwell)

A Christmas Carol (Charles Dickens)

A Midsummer Night's Dream
(William Shakespeare)

Alice, Alice in Wonderland and Alice
Through the Looking Glass (Lewis Carroll)

Alice on the Underground (Chris Bond)

The Ancient Mariner
(Samuel Taylor Coleridge)

Animal Farm (George Orwell)

The Resistable Rise of Arturo Ui
(Bertolt Brecht)

Badjelly's Bad Christmas (Spike Milligan)

Bazaar and Rummage (Sue Townsend)

The Beggar's Opera (John Gay)

Blood Wedding (Federico Garcia Lorca)

Brave New World (Aldous Huxley)

Bugsy (Alan Parker)

Can't Pay, Won't Pay! (Dario Fo)

The Caucasian Chalk Circle
(Bertolt Brecht)

Charlie and the Chocolate Factory
(Roald Dahl)

The Dot and the Line (Norton Juster)

The Government Inspector
(Nikolai Gogol)

The Grandfathers (Rory Mullarkey)

Grimm Nights and Everafter Days
(Brothers Grimm)

Gulliver (Jonathan Swift)

Hamlet (William Shakespeare)

If You're Glad, I'll Be Frank (Tom Stoppard)

The Insect Play (Karel and Josef Čapek)

In Watermelon Sugar (Richard Brautigan)

Journey to Jo'burg (Beverley Naidoo)

Killing Me Softly (David Yates)

The Laughing Man (Chris Bond)

Laundry Girls (Bill Owen)

Lord of the Flies (William Golding)

Love of Seven Dolls (Paul Gallico)

Lysistrata (Aristophanes)

Maid of Orleans (Friedrich Schiller)

The Night Before Christmas
(Clement Clarke Moore)

The Nutcracker and the Mouse King
(ETA Hoffmann)

Oh! What a Lovely War (Joan Littlewood)

Our Country's Good
(Timberlake Wertenbaker)

Pericles (William Shakespeare)

Peter Pan (JM Barrie)

Pinocchio (Carlo Collodi)

The Rite of Spring (Igor Stravinsky)

Romeo and Juliet and the Sonnets and
Soliloquies (William Shakespeare)

Sleeping Beauty
(Charles Perrault/Brothers Grimm)

Teechers (John Godber)

The Tempest (William Shakespeare)

Tom (Eleanor Farjeon)

Upon the Stones (David Yates)

Vanity Fair (William
Makepeace Thackeray)

Who's Afraid of Virginia's
Sister? (Sarah Daniels)

The Wizard of Oz (L Frank Baum)

The Would Be Gentleman
(F Anstey/Molière)

Yard Gal (Rebecca Prichard)

Badjelly's Bad Christmas, 2010.

Slender Threads, 2011.

Sleeping Beauty – Dream On, 2012.

MILESTONES

1974–2014

July 1974

Chrysalis: Lady Elizabeth Theatre Workshop, Norfolk Lodge Farm. The first show in the Chickenshed. The piece is workshopped and then performed.

1974

A group starts with thirty teenagers in a chicken shed on farmland.

1983

Introduction to Cheviots Children's Centre in Enfield.

Easter 1974

Isaac: The first show on which Jo, Mary and Anthony collaborate.

1982

Saturday Action: Chickenshed auditions for LWT and takes part in half of the series, with Jo writing a theme tune that is televised as the opening.

1987
December
Family Circle article
on Chickenshed in its
Christmas edition.

May 1988
Another side of London:
Thames TV make a
documentary. Media
interest increases.

1986
Company launches as
a charitable trust at the
Greedy Grape, Jo's wine bar.
Membership rises to 150.

1988
13 March
Judi Dench and Michael Williams host an
evening of Chickenshed. Brian McAndrew
(chief executive of London Borough of Enfield)
enlists the support of the Council to provide
premises for a workshop base. All those who
might help Chickenshed to get its own home
are invited. Crucially, Lord and Lady Rayne are
present and become supporters.

1989
5 December
Lady Rayne's first gala, Sadler's Wells (below). Introduced by Pauline Collins. Tom Conti also involved.

17 October 1990
Anansi at Sadler's Wells. First Royal Gala performance in the presence of Diana, Princess of Wales, who subsequently became Chickenshed's first royal patron.

October 1988
Preview of *Love of Seven Dolls* at Piccadilly Theatre.

1990
14 July
Anansi at the Royal Albert Hall (above). Chickenshed workshops and gathers a thousand children from twenty-two different London boroughs to perform. As a result Theatre in Inclusive Education (TIIE) continues in schools.

December 1990
Concert at the Hard
Rock Cafe, London. First
appearance at this venue.

12 December 1991
The Attraction at The Place.
Private visit by Diana,
Princess of Wales, and
Princes William and Harry.

14–17 November 1990
The Attraction at the
Shaw Theatre. First run in
Central London.

Above: Publicity shot
on the roof of the Shaw
Theatre with St Pancras
Station in the background.

1991
December
Performance on the *Wogan*
show at the BBC.

15 December 1991
Article by Matthew
Norman appears in the
Mail on Sunday.

The cast and backstage crew of *The Attraction* in rehearsal
for performance at the Shaw Theatre, 1990.

1992
January
Land provided by
Enfield Council on
peppercorn rent.

April 1992
John Bull seconded
from Enfield Council.

Left: Mary, Jo and
John's last-minute notes
in the dressing room.

December 1992
*The Night Before
Christmas* at The
Place, London.

1993
July
Paula's Story (above)
at Burford Hall.

1994
July
Filming of *We Need Each
Other* – a promotional
film in which Princess
Diana appears.

1995
7 May
Chickenshed performs at
the VE Day 50th Anniversary
celebrations in Hyde Park.

December 1994
The new Theatre opens.

November 1994
Filming of *Have a Heart*
at Christmas, Chickenshed's
Christmas single video.

19 December 1994
The Night Before Christmas at
Chickenshed Theatre Auditorium –
the first show at the new Theatre.

May–July 1995
The Attraction on tour
in Basildon, Wakefield,
Crewe and Swindon.

Right (left to right):
Martin Stone, Jody
Watson, Daniel Brearley,
Michele Durler and
Michael Charalambous.

1996
December
Mary Ward receives
the MBE for Services
to the Arts.

18 September 1995
BTEC starts, with the first of
Chickenshed's students.

1 December 1997
'I Am in Love with the World',
the Chickenshed single, is
included on a tribute album
in memory of the late Diana,
Princess of Wales.

15 December 1997
'I Am in Love with
the World' is released
as a single.

1997
4 March
Headline Publishing
celebrate the publication of
the book *Paula's Story*.

14 December 1997
Review of *A Christmas Carol*
on *Theatreland* on Channel 4.
Chickenshed first meets Bryan
Izzard (above).

23 December 1997
This Is Your Life episode
about Mary Ward,
recorded, and transmitted
on 29 December.

Right: Mary Ward, MBE.

Far right: Mary on *This Is
Your Life* with her husband,
Manus, and sons, Paddy
and Joe; and, above, with
Michael Aspel.

1998
October/November
Filming of *Christmas Day in the Morning* by LWT's *South Bank Show* to be broadcast on Christmas Day.

June 1999
Signing of partnership agreement with Middlesex University.

2002
May
Jo Collins receives the MBE for Services to Music (right).

1999
8 June
Official opening of new Chickenshed Theatre (above). Alan Howarth (minister for the arts) plants a tree to commemorate the day.

2000
19 July
Chickenshed performs at the Queen Mother's 100th birthday celebrations at Horse Guards Parade (above).

June 2002
Launch of MA in Lifelong Learning hosted by Lord David Puttnam (below).

4 June 2002
Chickenshed takes part in the Queen's Golden Jubilee parade on The Mall (above).

2003

Launch of 30th anniversary album, featuring Chickenshed celebrity supporters singing Chickenshed material.

2005

September

Chickenshed's first Foundation Degree course starts.

2007

July

Chickenshed's Children's Theatre performs at the Concert for Diana, Wembley Stadium, held in memory of Diana, Princess of Wales.

2008

7–8 May

'*as the mother of a brown boy ...*' (above) performed in the Rayne Theatre – Chickenshed's first issue-based production.

2009

7–30 August

Crime of the Century (below) and *Tales* performed at the Edinburgh Festival Fringe.

2012
February
Chickenshed performs at the Charles Dickens bicentenary celebrations (below) in the presence of the Queen and the Duke of Edinburgh.

2014
Chickenshed's 40th anniversary.

2010
April
Launch of Kensington and Chelsea Shed at Kensington Town Hall.

2013
November
The Hon. Natasha Rayne (above) hosts a Gala for the first time.

MUSICIANS AT CHICKENSHED

Youth bands over the years, often led by Michele Durler (top, second from left).

SOME OF OUR SUPPORTERS

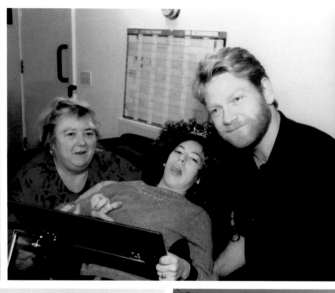

OUR VOLUNTEERS

Volunteers are the foundation stones on which Chickenshed is built

Each stone in this bucket represents a special person who has given their time, energy and enthusiasm to Chickenshed

These stones will be added to the foundations of the new shed

OUR FINAL VOTE OF THANKS...

Thank you to everyone who contributed their time, photos and stories,
and to our 40th anniversary sponsors, listed below.

Frank & Joy Hollick
1974

Chickenshed was born! Its amazing success is due to the dedication of the two people who conceived it.

The Rosalyn & Nicholas Springer Charitable Trust
1975

It has taken time to get from Roseberry Avenue to the Royal Albert Hall via Guildhall, but what a fabulous jouney.

Kate Varah
1976

In memory of Michael, who loved it. For Mary and Jo, who made it. With love and admiration.

Brit Trust
1977

A huge congratulations on your 40th year anniversary.

River Island
1978

Congratulations Chickenshed on forty years of outstanding creativity married with successful engagement and outreach across the whole community.

Friend
1979

At its best theatre is of, for and about the world we live in, made by those who live in it.

Daphne Dawes
1980

With best wishes for your 40th year.

Liz Reen
1981

In appreciation of the fantastic show *All I've Known* – a beautiful production.

The Gonzalez Family
1982

Inspirational, wonderful: Chickenshed. May it live on forever. Very much love. The Gonzalez family.

Alison Ritchie
1983

In memory of Peter Stevens 1981–2007. Chickenshed meant so much to him.

Sara & Paul Phillips
1984

In memory of my dear father, Norman Freed, who introduced us to the wonderful and life-changing work of Chickenshed.

Hard Rock
1985

A huge congratulations, Chickenshed – what an amazing achievement.

Mona • Monica, Stan & Jack Tourlamain
1986

Amazing – what an incredible journey.

Latifa Kosta
1987

Huge congratulations. With best wishes for your 40th year.

Ray & Clare Kelvin
1988

'You are an inspiration to us all.' In memory of our beloved Trudie Kelvin – 1926–2010.

Christine Mason
1989

Happy 40th birthday. It has been an honour to be a part of the incredible journey.

Belinda, Wendy & Stuart Sharer
1990

Inspired – Mary and Jo – create – CHICKENSHED, an uplifting enlightening celebration in this tantalising 40th anniversary book.

Lady Annabel Goldsmith
1991

Chickenshed is an inspiration to us all. I commend all of the hard work and enthusiasm that makes it the success it is today.

Galliard Group
1992

Galliard Group of Companies is delighted to be associated with Chickenshed and wish them continued success.

Laraine Krantz
1993

The year Anna joined, which changed our lives. I took my first photos at the Hard Rock and continue to do so, being moved emotionally and visually. Thank you!

EBM Charitable Trust
1994

The Trustees of the EBM Charitable Trust congratulate Chickenshed on their 40th anniversary.

The Heath Family
1995

Remembering Peter and Sally Heath, great supporters of Chickenshed.

Billy Allen
1996

Thank you Chickenshed for being in our lives through happy times and sad. Love from Jacquie, Jeff and Chanelle Allen.

Ralph Littlejohn, June Mitchell & Ruth Littlejohn
1997

For Ruth Littlejohn, with thanks to Chickenshed. A huge part of her life and a place she loves.

Sir Trevor Chinn
1998

With best wishes for your 40th year.

Mavis Forney
1999

In remembrance of Andrew Forney. A talented actor with Hampstead Garden Suburb Theatre, who died 17 November 1999 aged forty.

Janet Suzman
2000

For gallant and gifted and tireless Mary – without whom Chickenshed would not have happened.

Ernest Hecht
2001

The Ernest Hecht Charitable Foundation is proud to be a long-term supporter of Chickenshed's admirable work with diversity and inclusiveness.

Karen & Alex Midgen
2002

In memory of two special people: Rachel and David Shaw. You are missed every day that passes.

Dr Natalie Greenworld
2003

In loving memory of Natalie, Ben, Nathaniel and Phoebe.

Angela Soning
2004

I'd like to dedicate this year to all the amazing people I have met since my involvement with Chickenshed.

Mark & Helen Warren
2005

Nicole attended Chickenshed from 2005 providing her with motivation, confidence and ambition to perform throughout her teenage years.

Stephanie Press
2006

Member from 2005. Thank you Chickenshed for enriching my life and touching the hearts of so many people.

Derwent London PLC
2007

The merger between Derwent Valley and London Merchant Securities in 2007 reinforced our ongoing involvement and commitment to Chickenshed.

Tash & Delilah Rayne
2008

To the year that our paths crossed at FHS, which enriched our lives forever. AAAACMTX&Y.

DG Goldberg
2009

Many congratulations. With best wishes for your 40th year.

The Campsies
2010

Our best wishes. Thanks and love to an extraordinary place and group of people.

GM Real Estate
2011

We love Chickenshed!!!

Annie Sweetbaum
2012

Many congratulations on the amazing achievements over the last forty years.

Barry & Susan Denmead
2013

In memory of a remarkable mother, friend and mother-in-law.

For Martin Schwab
2014

How suitable that you and Chickenshed have joint birth years – you both bring energy, vitality and music wherever you go! Happy 40th! C, T & X.

OUR STUDENTS

BTEC 1997–2013

1997

1998

1999

2000

2001

2002

2003

2004

2005

2006

2007

2008

2009

2010

2011

2012

2013

FOUNDATION DEGREE 2007–2013 • BA DEGREE 2013

2007

2008

2009

2010

2011

2012

2013

BA · 2013

OUR STUDENTS 1997–2013

BTEC 1997–2013

1997: Anthony Adjekum, Ruth Collins, Edwin Din, James Dunbar, Ben Gardner, Vince Goss, Andy James, Jason Percival, Nadine Ruddock, Maurice Sampson, Rebecca Seabrook, Belinda Sharer, Joanne Smith, Darren Sparks, Theresa Vincent, Yvonne Voegt, Adam Youngman

1998: Maher Al-Aride, Bradley Baum, Nicola Bleasdale, Rukiya Burress, Chris Christou, Kim Cooper, Lewis Davis, Mary-Ellen Flatley, Caroline Hoare, Vanya Hooshue, Dean James, Senel Karava, Ali Latif, Elisa Lord, Jzules Maharaj, Lesley Miles, Chloe Misson, Katie Mitchell, Sarah Plunkett, Dervis Purodron, Romany Rix, Suzan Sinem Salih, Zein Suheimat, Michelle Wright

1999: Adil Aourarh, Nimal Ariyadasa, Clive Boxall, Daniel Cowan, Joanna Crossman, Jarrard Curtis, Akin Goksel, Clare Greenland, Sam Harper, Vicky Hawkins, Patrick Holbrook, Jamie Horgan, Carina Ioannou, Zarina Jeans, Louisa Jenkins, Desi Joseph, Paul Kent, Roshan Kodabuckus, Elizabeth Lomotey, Stavros Louca, Patrick Murray, Neil Ross, Davina Sanders, Amanda Siaw, Diane Smitherman, Linda Soper, Paul Storan, Dan Waller, Gregory Williams

2000: Kellie Archer, Daniel Barnett, Frederick Benfield, Geoffrey Boud, Shareen Dean, Joanne Dobson, Gemma Franco, Peter Griffin, Natsai Gurupira, Dawn Jackson, Elizabeth Jones, Orli Josephs, Princess Mannah, Andre Morgan, Michael Offei, Mary Pilastiros, Louise Reen, Naomi Sparrow, Johnathon Stoute, Leila Tanner, Aylin Tuncer

2001: Anthony Andrews, Emily Bagshaw, Samantha Burniston, Victoria Chapman, Simon Cooper, Bruno David, Natalie Davidson, Alexander Demetriades, Athena Demetriou, Errol Drysdale, Antonia Edwards, Sam Frears, Alison Grey, Chantelle Harris, Sarah Jerome, Naomi Locker, Christie Michael, Anthony Muriithi, Alexandra Nadel, Ventris Obeney, Tomislav Pavlinic, Laura Pettitt, Christina Sammoutis, Natalie Taylor, Ross Taylor, Wesley Taylor

2002: Sophie Adams, Christopher Andreou, Olivia Banks, Sam Bayley, Joseph Casulli, Tommy Doyle, Sevda Durmush, Bobbi Eaton, Chinemelu Ezigbo, Glen Fox, Toby Gillingham, Amy Golden, Carla Iannacone, Stephanie Lane, Jessica Lee, Fae Lyons, Mark McKenzie, Edward Mosse, Alexander Ness, Priyanda Patel, Maria Payne, Vathoulla Pitsillides, Elliot Rosen, Victoria Smith, Leschell Wright

2003: Ellie Boltman, Anna Brooks-Beckman, Emma Cambridge, Tom Cameron, Katie Caryer, Anthony Clarke, Rebecca Cooper, Esther Finn, Lucy Harris, Lissa Hermans, Clive Heslop, Junaid Jackson, Roxanne Jacobs, Andrew Joannou, Adam Karayiannis, Ben Lee, Mark Lees, Christina Linsey, Joseph Lucas, Laura Meldrum, Lizzie Mellor, Sofia Nakitende, Antonia Rosenthal, Katie Russell, Tessa Ryan, Martin Sherlock, Clare Simper, Attey Sonkour, Amy Taylor, Sam White, Alexander Yau

2004: Jake Arditti, Daniel Banton, Chris Berry, Michael Bossisse, Lauren Cambridge, Delwyn Charlemagne, Holly Cheyne, Kelly-Denise Curran, Sam Davis, Claire Day, Jenny Fowler, George Gavas, Gina Giles, Leo Howard, Pascha Hudson, Samantha Jacobs, Anusha Jakubowska, Justine Johnson, Ottilie Kark, Lindsey Knight, Sabiha Kulle, Emma Kunicki, Camilla Linton-Marcel, Howard Martin, Gavin May, Demetra Petrou, Rachel Puleston, Natalie Russo, Clare Stevenson, Josh Viner, Angelica-Blaise Williams

2005: Helen Adams, Skender Allamani, Rebecca Allen, Chiso Anyanwu, Charlotte Barnett, Steven Berman, Hayley Burns, Gemma Crabb, Shireena Crawley, Guner Dopran, Amanda George, Daniel Gonzalez, Khalid Ibrahim, Nadia Ismail, Chris January, Christie Joannou, Robert Johnson, Emily-Jane Kent, Lincoln Kyei, Ruth Littlejohn, Josh Lyth, Paula MacGregor, Jenny McCaffrey, Zengani Mhone, Sabrina Mottram, Tara O'Donnell-Brown, Georgie Reading, Ileana Ribeiro, Pralathan Sivagnanam, Andy Taylor, Chloe-Amber Thomas, Kerri-Anne Wakefield

2006: Ardit Alihakaj, Annique Appadoo, Craig Baxter, Verity Butcher, Katy Carter, Dominique Crooks, Jamie Demetriou, Diambote Ditoma, Katie Flexman, Dominic Garfield, Michael Hagan, Jack Hoskins, Tania Jacobs, Tara Jacobs, Holly Jones, Zoe Kennedy, John Livingston, Ashley Maynard, Stacey McKnight, Kayleigh Mitcham, Chidimma Otuonye, Tamika Phillip, Eliane Powell, Laura Rojas, Francesca Spicer, Holly Sturgess, Elizabeth Thompson, Joleigh Wynter, Alev Yilmaz

2007: Chanelle Allen, Stacey Allison, Simone Barnes, Dervise Beyzade, Katya Bradford, Sam Campbell, Natasha Colleemallay, Sarah Connolly, Philip Constantinou, Maxeen Crowley, Laura Davitt, Stephanie Dye, Nadia Hamilton, Gary Jenkins, Klara Kalvelage, Charlie Kervons, Jenna Lewis, Mahalia Lloyd, Sylvie Maher, Luke Mappoura, Sarah McLellan, Danyle Morris, Daniel Norie, Kathleen Phillips, Christina Picton, Murat Shevket, Sarah Vidowsky

2008: Bercem Birol, Cesare Cascarino, Michaela Charalambous, Sophia Cordell, Lindsay Craig, Ayten Dagli, Bradley Davis, Louise de Spon, Aeren Fitzgerald, Adam Griffin, Sam Griffiths, Luke Hards, Adrian Harper, Thomas Herreboudt, Rebecca Humphreys, Lucy Jarosy, Rhea Jarvis, Ozan Koc, Aliky Kolovos, Adam Krstic, Tania Lock,

Emilie-Mae MacCormack, Kelly Milligan, Myles Morgan, Jan Pekozkay, Ravi Rajkumar, Kerstin Simpson, Sally Trevette, Kimberley Van der Velde, Sarah Ward, Nathan Williams

2009: Nana Amma Addo-Gyamfi, Emily Arnold, Alisah Atmaca, Sarah Brewer, Marcus Christian, Jayde Christian, Joanna Cooper, Chantal Dias, James Dulay-Jefferson, Paul Fricker, Lee Geohagen, Rory Graham, Marisa Hadgitheologou, Paul Harris, Ashley Hawkins, Natalia Hyson, Claire Johnas, Sarah Jones, William Laurence, Charlotte Lee, Shayla Lowe, Kayleigh Marchant, Danielle Martin, Chelsea Mason, Erol Mustafa, Amrut Patel, Marc Picard, Beth Revan, Gemilla Shamruk, Alice Sidell-Hodgson, Lauren Surridge, Lynda-Louise Tomlinson, Ian Wagner, Anna Williams

2010: Shaleka Black-Heaven, Michaela Blanchard, Sophie Chappell, Natasha Curran, Misha Daniels, Simon Degen, Rosie Driscoll, Charlotte Duncombe, Oliver Fernandez, Adriana Fleisher, Charlie Hampshire, Bianca Harris, Tom Harvey, Nathan Hector, Sanya Hurlock, James Ketteridge, Anna-Louise Leyden, Georgina McGuirk, Meliz Mehmet, Constantina Menezes, Emily Moran, Paola Muratori, Arian Sadeghi, Shradha Savani, Brooke Smith, Gemma Terry, Jodie Tierney, Katherine Walker, Becky White, Jerell William, Carmel Woodbridge

2011: Billy Ashworth, Jeylan Bhola, Bethany Bullman, Jodie Clarke, Hayley Cox, Josh Cramer-Smer, Tinashe Crooks, Akaash Darji, Rebecca Dolan, Jessica Dynevor, Tiffany Gaine, Kyri Georgiou, Helen Harris, Sabah Hussein, Luke Johnson, Sophie Kaytaz, Shanel Koroglu, Jem Nedjib, Charles Oni, Alex Pendakis, Luke Ricketts, Danielle Roznoski, Antonia Sergiou, Anthony Sexton, Rebecca Singh, Athena Sofroniou, Alex Theoharous, Rosie Vachat, Sarah Vinning, Leo White, Nathaniel Xavier

2012: Enzi Alexander, Panny Apostoli, Benjamin Bland, Shannay Bramwell, Salih Cikikcioglu, Jasmin Clarke, Kate Clavey, Mary Cole, Ben Dye, Antonia Economides, Zack Field, Amy Green, Amy Gurnell, Lauren Haines, Sorcha Hannon, Rebecca Hindle, Sandra Horvathova, Jermaine Ivers, Jessica Konzon, Katerina Makri, Ben Moody, Anita O-Koleosho, Eddie Palmer, Emine Pasa, Goutham Rohan, Zoe Roseweir, Michaela Shaw, Michaela Silverstein, Sophia Stavrou, Zahra Welle, George Wood

2013: Mazlum Altun, Jerry Balintuma, Josh Brennan, Lauren Butterfield, Munise Cevik, George Christodoulou, Ella Cove, Paige Cowell, Nathan Crosby-Pinnock, Daniela Danielewicz, Charlotte Doe, Jessica Dynevor, Charles Edelsten, Eva Gibbs, Lauren Karstadt, Sina Kavoussian, Tara Kleanthous, Jordan Kouame, James Le Dain, Luke Mallett, Adam Mann, Hope Marks, Kathleen McDonagh, Sade Morrall, Michelle Nachum, Mehdi Ourabah, Emma Pallett, Jessica Ratcliffe, Kyle Rees-Blackstone, Toby Sams-Friedman, Curtis Stephen, Jennifer Wilcox

FOUNDATION DEGREE

2007: Rebecca Allen, Charlotte Barnett, Steven Berman, Jessica Clipp, George Gavas, Gina Giles, Lucy Harris, Robert Johnson, Mark Lees, Josh Lyth, Gavin May, Georgie Reading, Andy Taylor

2008: Daniel Banton, Natasha Beyer, Michael Bossisse, Emma Cambridge, Michael Gavas, Michael Hagan, Tania Jacobs, Zoe Kennedy, Ashley Maynard, Louisa Ozongwu, Tessa Ryan

2009: Chanelle Allen, Katya Bradford, Lauren Cambridge, Katy Carter, Ellie Connolly, Sarah Connolly, Dominique Crooks, Laura Davitt, Stephanie Dye, Jack Hoskins, Klara Kalvelage, Mahalia Lloyd, Danyle Morris, Daniel Norie, Rosea Pickering, Murat Shevket, Sarah Vidowsky

2010: Emma Balaam, Michaela Charalambous, Philip Constantinou, Bradley Davis, Aeren Fitzgerald, Sam Griffiths, Luke Hards, Adrian Harper, Rebecca Humphreys, Lucy Jarosy, Myles Morgan, Kenny Nicolson, Anthony Pickersgill, Kerstin Simpson, Rebecca Uings, Nathan Williams

2011: Nana Amma Addo-Gyamfi, Emily Arnold, Alice Chambers, Louise de Spon, James Dulay-Jefferson, Lee Giles, Paul Harris, Natalia Hyson, Tara Jacobs, Claire Johnas, William Laurence, Charlotte Lee, Laura Meldrum, JoJo Morrall, Erol Mustafa, Marc Picard, Gemilla Shamruk, Paige Stubley, Lynda-Louise Tomlinson, Sally Trevette

2012: Sophie Chappell, Kerry Conley, Sophia Cordell, Natasha Curran, Simon Degen, Rosie Driscoll, Charlotte Duncombe, Adriana Fleisher, Paul Fricker, Marvin Hamilton-Chambers, Tom Harvey, Sarah Jones, James Ketteridge, Anna Knight, Georgina McGuirk, Alice Sidell-Hodgson, Brooke Smith, Gemma Terry, Katherine Walker, Becky White, Jerell William

2013: Jeylan Bhola, Bethany Bullman, Jodie Clarke, Samantha Corrway, Katy Cracknell, Josh Cramer-Smer, Tinashe Crooks, Rebecca Dolan, Susan Horsup, Sabah Hussein, Sophie Kaytaz, Blossom McDonagh, Grace Muter, Charles Oni, Regan O'Reilly, Alex Pendakis, Beth Revan, Luke Ricketts, Sarah Vinning, Anna Williams, Carmel Woodbridge

BA DEGREE

2013: Shakira Badley, Sophie Chappell, Jayde Christian, Kerry Conley, Natasha Curran, Bradley Davis, Dominique Davis, Rosie Driscoll, James Dulay-Jefferson, Charlotte Duncombe, Adriana Fleisher, Paul Fricker, Tom Harvey, Sarah Jones, James Ketteridge, Anna Knight, William Laurence, Georgina McGuirk, Laura Meldrum, Kate Meranda, Gemilla Shamruk, Gemma Terry, Katherine Walker

INDEX

Page numbers in *italic* refer to illustrations.

ACKNOWLEDGEMENTS

Mary and Jo would like to say here and now and hopefully to be remembered
forever, the hugest, humblest and eternally grateful *thank you* to all of the
following, and anyone else falling outside of these groups:

Our wonderful staff, past and present – full-time, part-time and sometime! – who work the longest and most devoted hours of their lives.

Our amazing volunteers past and very much present, without whom we would not be able to exist. Heaven knows what their contribution would amount to financially – probably millions of pounds!

Our personal friends and families who have unquestioningly (most of the time!) supported our every move.

The monks of Christ the King, the Cockfosters Benedictine Monastery, who have been inspirational both spiritually and practically.

Our trusty trustees and gala patrons who have always supported us and continue to do so.

Enfield Council, all schools, colleges and establishments with whom we've worked.

All our members and students, past and present. You are *why* we are!

Our loyal parents, audiences, celebrities, funders – both individuals and grant giving bodies – corporate and general supporters – please don't ever stop!

Our author, Liz, our publishers, Jennie, Olivia and James, and Jeannette, who managed the project.

And finally, our two patrons – firstly the late Lady Elizabeth Byng and then the late Diana, Princess of Wales.

And *everyone* else who has taken this ride with us. Please stay on board for the next forty!

Jo and Mary